# ONBOARDING

## Strategies for getting employees up to speed faster

### Dr Charles du Toit

TALENT MANAGEMENT SERIES

First published in 2019.

ISBN: 978-1-86922-816-3
eISBN: 978-1-86922-817-0 (ePDF)

Published by KR Publishing
P O Box 3954
Randburg
2125
Republic of South Africa

Tel: (011) 706-6009
Fax: (011) 706-1127
E-mail: orders@knowres.co.za
Website: www.kr.co.za

Typesetting, layout and design: Cia Joubert, cia@knowres.co.za
Cover design: Marlene de'Lorme, marlene@knowres.co.za
Editing and proofreading: Valda Strauss, valda@global.co.za
Project management: Cia Joubert, cia@knowres.co.za

# Table of Contents

## About the author

Prior to his current role as the CEO of Dr Charles du Toit and Associates, a niche Leadership and HR consultancy, Dr Charles du Toit was the HR Director of Eveready in South Africa for 16 years. Today he provides leadership development solutions, training and strategic support to a wide range of significant corporations and several Business Schools. He is also the founder and chairperson of the Nelson Mandela Bay HR Forum. Charles currently holds a PhD in Leadership through Change from the University of Johannesburg.

# Introduction

It is said that you only really get to understand the importance of something you are involved in when you have distance from it. In my case, this book reflects two areas of personal discovery after the event.

Having worked for a range of leading multinationals, I found myself leading the HR function of a local iconic, but small, South African company. While our HR department had limited resources, we were able to achieve some exciting initiatives. The leadership culture we created was unique and treasured by all in the organisation.

During this time, because of the resignation of a new start, we were challenged to improve our induction programme. Our HR team brainstormed a solution and came up with an approach which was unique some 15 years ago – a five-stage induction programme. We only discovered some time later that this was called "Onboarding". At the time, we were just keen to use induction to build our leadership culture.

Some seven years later I registered for research in the field of Leadership. The focus of my study was the role of HR in creating a leadership brand within an organisation. This was influenced, at the time, by Dave Ulrich and John Smallwood's, book *Leadership Brand*.[1] My research showed that the HR department has a critical role to play in creating the environment where leadership thrives and a leadership culture emerges.

This role, however, is often missed by HR practitioners, as well as theorists. HR's role goes beyond nurturing leadership development. Many of the key HR functions, such as organisational design, recruitment, Onboarding, training and development, industrial relationships and succession planning could be just HR functions, or they could be viewed as strategic initiatives which all contribute to the enablement of the leadership culture.

It is our experience that, increasingly, leadership is gaining centre stage in organisational strategy. The work that I now do is focused on building leadership capability across organisations. Often, during my discussions, Onboarding has come up as an area of organisational concern.

Therefore, this book looks at Onboarding as much more than just one of the things an HR department does. Onboarding, from our perspective, is the first step of the leadership relationship. Great Onboarding requires the commitment of the entire organisational leadership.

Strategic Onboarding is seen as an important part of the process of building the leadership culture of an organisation. Therefore, investing time and energy in doing this well, makes sense. I hope you enjoy working through this book as much as I did writing it.

## Who is this book for?

This book is intended for HR leaders, HR Business Partners and line leaders across the spectrum of organisational leadership from CEO to line leader. This book is also of use to leaders and employees who are about to transition into new positions.

HR leaders and business practitioners who are responsible for Onboarding will find practical implementation ideas around how to design, craft and sell Onboarding to line leaders, and implement an effective Onboarding process.

Onboarding must be the first step of leadership. Line leaders therefore play a vital role in ensuring that Onboarding is implemented effectively. Ultimately, they are the benefactors of an effective Onboarding process and thus would benefit from looking at the different dimensions in Onboarding.

Employees who are about to start a new position, especially employees who are about to start in a new leadership position, should also benefit from reflecting on the Onboarding process. While Onboarding is a company leadership imperative, new starts, irrespective of the internal organisational structures, would benefit from effectively Onboarding themselves. This book will provide great insight into how this can be achieved.

While this book is about Onboarding, it has an underpinning leadership theme. To really benefit from Onboarding, it must be the first step towards leadership.

I have made use of the two genders interchangeably in the book to avoid any perception of gender bias. In addition, I have included a generic succession process that you can adapt and customise based on your needs.

## Using this book

This book follows the Onboarding flow chart illustrated on page vi and outlines four main areas of focus. These are: Building an argument and support for Onboarding; Introducing the new employee to the company; Becoming organisationally competent; and Onboarding leaders.

We identify five Onboarding imperatives, or the Why? of Onboarding. They are the speed at which an employee is brought to full performance, the new employee's psychological contract with the organisation, the impact of the new employee on company image in the market, introducing the new employee to the team and finally the second major theme, the leadership relationship which may emerge throughout the process.

# Flowchart for Onboarding

| | Chapter 1: | Chapter 2: | Chapter 3: |
|---|---|---|---|
| **Building an argument and support for Onboarding** | Why Onboarding? The argument for a professional Onboarding process. | A comprehensive Onboarding process. A 5-stage Onboarding process, from signing on to company competent. | How to get started. How to build internal support for a comprehensive Onboarding process. |

| | Chapter 4: | | Chapter 5: |
|---|---|---|---|
| **The process of introducing in a new employee** | Land the fish. Ensuring that a newly recruited employee is prepared for their introduction into a new organisation. | | The first days. Ensuring that an employee's first days leave a positive first impression. |

| | Chapter 6: | Chapter 7: | Chapter 8: |
|---|---|---|---|
| **The process of building company competency** | Getting to know the giant. Assisting the new employee to get to know their employer's entire business. | Who is who in the Zoo. Assisting the new employee to become part of the team. | Becoming company competent. Assisting the new employee to acquire the competencies to function fully in their new company. |

| | Chapter 9: | | Chapter 10: |
|---|---|---|---|
| **Inducting a new leader and pulling it all together** | Onboarding when there is a particular challenge facing a new leader. Building Leadership influence. | | Conclusion. Taking a final look at the value of Onboarding. |

# Chapter 1

## Why Onboarding?

*The argument for a professional Onboarding process.*

## Introduction

If you are reading this book the chances are that you already feel that, when it comes to Onboarding, there is room for improvement. I am interested in your own personal experience. In my research for this book I could not find anyone who felt that their Onboarding experiences could be written up as best practice. In fact, most people I spoke to reflected that their experience when joining a company was a disaster. Why would that be?

Why would we neglect the most basic of business processes, i.e. getting a new start up and running as soon as possible? Surely we would want the new start to be ready to perform, become part of the team and add huge value as quickly as possible. Surely that is why we recruited them in the first place. Why, when a new person starts, would we not already know their names or have their computers ready? Why would we feel the need to overwhelm them with rules and safety talks rather than getting to know them?

Who is responsible to see that this new entrant is successful? Is this an HR function or something line leadership should take on as their responsibility? This is the place where the HR practitioner is extremely vulnerable. It is so easy to turn to the HR team and raise an eyebrow when a new start has had a very bumpy entrance into the company.

As the "war for talent" rages and the global perspective that talent is not geographically grounded increases, ensuring that our organisations become good at Onboarding is more than a basic management function; it is an area of competitive advantage. In this book we take a deeper look at Onboarding and provide a framework for a world-class Onboarding process.

We differentiate between Onboarding and induction – induction being the process of equipping the employee with the very basic knowledge they require to get started with Onboarding which, for us, is only really completed when the new start is really on board.

Onboarding takes place across three dimensions:

**Onboard psychologically**
**"a functioning member of the team"**

**Onboard functionally**
**"doing the job which they were recruited to do at the standard that is expected"**

**Onboard culturally**
**"aligned to the company culture and values"**

For us the term "Onboarding" creates the mental picture of people coming on board an ancient sailing boat. In other words, leaving the safety of one boat, making their way across a stretch of ocean with all the perils of a stormy sea, and boarding a new vessel.

---

**Arno's story:**

*When I first met Arno I was really impressed with his young, massive, positive energy and his passion for what he does at his company. He has been earmarked for a senior position in the future, and it is already evident that he will make a significant contribution. But it was not always so. Arno's entry into the company was shocking. During a training programme Arno attended, I asked members of the class to reflect on their Onboarding experiences. I could immediately see that I had hit a nerve. Arno became extremely agitated and almost aggressive. Then the story poured out.*

---

*Arno was recruited out of Agriculture College by a large blue-chip Agri Processing company. He reflected that he was extremely proud to have been selected and was even more proud that he had been appointed to take up the position as the company representative in a very active agricultural centre. His appointment meant that he would move to the small town in the middle of the area and head up the office which had pride of place on the main street. Arno had grown up in a similar farming community, so he thought he understood the dynamic.*

*The day before his first day at work, he drove some 500 km to his new home town and moved into a Bed and Breakfast which the company had provided for a month in order to get him settled. The following day, dressed in his best suit, he arrived at the office. As he walked in, the administrator looked up over the desk and stared at him for a moment and then asked if she could help. When he told her who he was, he could see the panic in her face. She clearly had not expected him, but she could guess that this young man, the same age as her own child, was her new boss.*

*She told him to come in and wait in the small reception area. She disappeared, clearly trying to find out what was going on. After an hour she came back and told Arno that Frikkie, the person he was replacing, had been working in the office for 30 years and, having reached retirement, was now going on pension at the coast. He would not be in that day because the golf club was having a function in his honour. In fact, he was playing the 6$^{th}$ hole as they spoke. She told Arno that he should not worry as Frikkie was going to be in the next day and had planned to be in the office for the next three days to show him the ropes. She suggested that he go back to the guest house and return the following day.*

*Arno reflected on how his first day would be the worst day of his entire career. The rest of the week was not much better. The following day Frikkie indeed came in and Arno was told to sit in the office and learn from Frikkie. For the next two days, apart from two very long lunch breaks, Arno watched Frikkie take phone call after phone call from members of the community who were obviously very fond of Frikkie and sad that he was leaving town.*

*By the time Frikkie had left, Arno had received no instruction on how he was supposed to operate, who his major clients were, or even what the company's expectations were. Arno did not even know who he was reporting to until, about a week later, Frank arrived to enquire why the sales report had not been sent in on time.*

## Who is responsible for the Onboarding process?

This is an important question. In most organisations HR is viewed as the custodian of the Onboarding process. This is often simply because HR is the custodian of all people processes. While the size of an organisation and the level of sophistication residing in the HR department will determine the extent of the impact that HR have on this process, there are three fundamental questions worth examining.

- Who is ultimately responsible for the employee?

- Whose interest is served in speedily Onboarding an employee?

- Whose leadership is reflected in the Onboarding process?

It is obvious that while HR may have some role to play in this process, Onboarding must ultimately be a line management responsibility.

*Just from a practical point of view, the average ratio of HR personnel to employees, varies between 1: 150 to 1: 300+. If you exclude the administrative HR functions, these ratios are much wider. What impact can such an HR person have on the day-to-day Onboarding process of a new employee? At best they can plan a well executed induction day.*

Line managers, though, may say they don't have time for this stuff; they have "sales to make" or "production to run". This sentiment is very old fashioned. Essentially such a sentiment amounts to:

### "I don't have time to lead, I'm too busy managing."

Does this mean that HR does not have a role in the "Onboarding process"? Of course not!! Best practice seems to be that HR can provide:

- A framework for the organisation.

- Auditing of the effectiveness of the process.

- Interviewing new starts and tracking their Onboarding experience.

- Training and prompting of line leaders in Onboarding,

- Supporting and simplifying the administrative process.

- Some generic training in company policies and health and safety.

- Initiating the provision of equipment, including office, uniform and computers.

The effective Onboarding of a new employee must be in the line leader's best interest and is therefore a critical part of their role.

> It is our belief that the committed line leader should naturally be committed and passionate about every stage of the Onboarding process for the many reasons we will unpack below.

## Why should we pay attention to the Onboarding process?

Onboarding is a business term which is probably 15 years old and it has become an increasing focus, because previous terms, such as induction or initiation, have a very limited scope.

The difference between Onboarding and the previous approaches is that bringing a new employee "on board" is a significant process, not a single event, which was the new employee's experience in the past.

As our view of the importance of the individual in a corporation has shifted, so has our need to improve the processes we used to integrate them into our companies properly. Proper Onboarding has several distinct and strategic purposes. Let's look at them for a moment:

The diagram shows "Onboarding Drivers" surrounded by:
- Speed and cost
- Employee value proposition
- Building a team
- The leadership moment
- The psychological contract

## Speed and cost

In this context speed and costs are two tightly linked components. We may not like it, but let's be honest, our people cost money and we have an organisational responsibility to realise this cost into value as soon as possible. From day one we pay our new employee at full value for full performance, but it is very unlikely that a new employee will be able to perform at full performance for a long time. I have heard people reflect that it could take one year or more before an employee in a complex job will be fully functional. This could amount to a significant real, but hard-to-measure, cost.

The reality is that until a new employee is fully functional, their role is either being neglected or someone else will be doing the job, as well as their own. Clearly, this is not ideal and therefore a strong case for effective and carefully planned "Onboarding".

There are several other speed-related drivers you may not have considered, but which are great reasons for getting the new start up and running as soon as possible. These include:

■ The obvious burden on existing employees.

■ The speed at which we develop new customer relationships.

■ The ability to focus on adding value to the new position rather than just coping.

■ The psychological impact on the new start's confidence when he/she can do the job properly.

■ Impact on the leaders' KPIs of below-required performance.

All the above relate to the value of speed. But this is not the only area driving a case for an effective "Onboarding" process.

## Building the psychological contract

Research shows that we all delay building a perception about something until we have enough experience to make an informed decision. We tend to give it the benefit of the doubt until we have clear evidence to the contrary. When the Onboarding process is effective it should go a long way in building the psychological contract between the employee and their new company. New hires could respond to great Onboarding as follows:

■ "This organisation has my best interests at heart."

■ "Wow, they really make me feel valued."

■ "This is so different to how my previous company treated me/ new people."

■ "There is something special about this place."

Alternatively, if I feel as if I am just a number and disposable, it is likely that I will begin to develop a deep sense of cynicism.

Think about how you would have felt about your new company if your Onboarding experience was the same as Arno's. As many new employees' first impressions of the Onboarding process are poor, it goes without saying that this has a potentially significant impact on the psychological contract between employee and company.

After a poor Onboarding experience it is possible that the employee would respond like this:

- "If this is how they treat new people, how will they treat me when they have to make a call about my future?"
- "This company is no better than the one I left."
- "Their sales pitch during the interview and the reality are completely different. I wonder what else they are not honest about."

Stephen Covey (*The Seven Habits of Highly Effective People*)[2] uses the metaphor of "Emotional Bank Account". He spoke about building a positive investment in the lives of our people. This starts the moment a new start has signed the contract. We know that having an engaged workforce is critical to organisational culture. Well, it stands to reason that we begin building engagement from the moment the employee joins up.

## Building the employee value proposition

These days it is common to hear people speak about employers they would like to work for and other employers they would not. This is even more common when recruiting employees from the "XY and Z" Generations. In the modern war for talent, investing in the image a company has in the marketplace, is increasingly becoming a competitive advantage issue. We call this the Employee Value Proposition (EVP).

It stands to reason that the Onboarding process is a great EVP moment. When you start at a new company you are very likely to be a "great advert" for your new employer. If the experience is great, everyone you know will be interested in your new position and company. The new start is very motivated to tell everyone about how great the decision is to move or take up the position.

We have the tendency to see only the good in a choice we have made, and we actively promote our decisions with others. This is a psychological occurrence that we call the "Choice-Supportive Bias." It has been well researched and as a consequence our new employee could be our best advert. While this would work in many circumstances, think how it could in the graduate space.

*An Engineering graduate joins a new company and reports back to peers that the company is awesome, relays some exciting experiences, and reflects that he feels very comfortable with the decision made. One evening in the pub and all other 4th year engineers will begin to take this company seriously as a future employer.*

The converse is unfortunately also true. While the "Choice-Supportive bias" would normally click in, if the experience is the same as Arno's – really bad – and the new employee develops a really strong cynical view of the company early, your "Arnos" could end up quickly destroying your image in the recruitment market place without you even knowing it.

## Building a team

Apart from the speed of coming to full performance and individual commitment, introducing a new member to a team has an impact on the other members of the team. Core to the leadership challenge of bringing a new member into a team, is the ability to build the relationship between team members based on trust.

Since the 60s we have been referring to the Tuchman model of building a high-performance group. Forming, storming, norming and performing. While this model works well for a group in the workplace, each time we introduce a new member to the team we reboot this process. When a team loses an existing member, it loses part of its legacy. The extent of this loss is linked to all sorts of factors, but once a new start has been brought in, the socialisation process starts all over again:

- Form – where the new star is welcomed,
- Storm – the adjustment process as a new personality struggles to find its place in an existing group,
- Norm – where the rhythm of the team's activities settles down and, if we are lucky,
- Perform – where the team begins to display the superpowers a high-performance team is recognised for: great results, innovation, flexibility and resilience among others.

We need to get the team back as quickly as possible to performing. An effective Onboarding process is critical to re-establishing the team to full performance. Our new start, as well as the team they join, will need to move through the four stages again. If we are deliberate and carefully plan the new start's entry, we can get back to the norming performing level as soon as possible.

## The leadership moment

Grace Hopper[3] set the tone for our thinking on Leadership and Onboarding: "We manage things, we lead people." An Onboarding process is all about our new people and how we lead them; they surely are not just a "thing" we manage. Onboarding a new employee is much more than a business process. This is the first act of leadership. The first step is building a leader–subordinate relationship, and this is a critical one.

If Onboarding is a great experience for the new employee, the employee is very likely to begin to develop trust in the leader. A good experience will communicate demonstrably to the follower that:

- The leader really cares.
- The leader is concerned for the follower's wellbeing.
- The leader has the follower's best interests at heart.
- It also communicates that the leader can put a good plan together.

**Let's have a quick look at modern leadership thinking in this context.**

Most modern theories define leadership in the same way as the "ability of an individual to influence other individuals and groups of individuals towards a common goal" (Northouse).[4]

It stands to reason that from the follower perspective, if I as the follower experience my leader as capable and having my best interests at heart, it is very likely that I will begin to develop trust in you. Developing trust is an important step in the modern leader/follower relationship.

The converse is also true; if Onboarding is neglectful, the experience probably leaves serious doubts in the follower's mind regarding the value and importance the leader attributes to the follower. Therefore, it will be even more difficult for the leadership–follower trust relationship to emerge.

Is this important? Well, yes, although the leader has positional power and can achieve results through demanding compliance. While this power-based management style is a more common approach to management, this is not leadership. At least, not leadership in the modern context. Not leadership that achieves the spectacular results that are possible when the leader begins to influence great results.

tips/ideas

*If you trust your leader and the leader suggests a direction, the follower is likely to follow.*

*The ability to get people to follow you is what we call influence, and trust is accepted as the crucial ingredient needed for the leader to gain authentic influence.*

### The out-of-date myth: "Sink or Swim"
### "Throw them in the deep end."

Do you really think dropping a child into a swimming pool and seeing them sink at first, only to pop up screaming, after a few breath-taking moments, is the best way to teach a child to swim? The phrase "sink or swim" has origins back to the 13th century. In the 21st century we have surely moved on a little. Only for the most inhumane parent in the modern day is the "Sink or Swim" method considered the best way of teaching children to swim. Does that mean that the "Sink or Swim" method did not work? No. In fact, a child's instinct for self-preservation is so strong that in "most cases" the child survives.

"Sink or Swim" worked in the context that rather than drown, the child would miraculously find in itself the ability to float.

If your objective is to encourage survival, then yes, maybe this really worked. If your objective is deeper than that it will be to build a love for the water and for swimming. It will be to expose a child to an environment that is full of fun and adventure and to build confidence in that environment where young bodies are safe and can play for hours. If you have a deeper intention it is unlikely that giving the child a life-threatening experience at the start will achieve the desired result.

### With "Sink or Swim" we run the risk of scaring
### away the child's desire to swim forever.

If this is true, and research says it is so, why would we think that "Sink or Swim" is an effective modern "Onboarding practice?" Why, if you ask around, do you hear so many stories of disastrous Onboardings where new starts are given limited or no support when they start in a new position?

*"Sink or Swim" is at best an excuse for management neglect and at worst an abusive practice which defines a workplace bully rather than a leader.*

## Conclusion

We see Onboarding as far more than the common view of what happens during the first day at work during induction. The objective of effective Onboarding should be that the new start is fully integrated into the organisation and is able to, at least, function at the level envisaged at the time of appointment. This is the level at which the previous incumbent was performing (if there was a previous incumbent who was able to perform at an optimal level and contributed as a high-performance team member).

For us, of at least equal importance is the notion that:

### "Onboarding is an important first act of leadership"

During the following chapters we will unpack the Onboarding process in some detail. To do this we have developed a five-stage model of Onboarding. Each stage has a specific objective and outcome and each stage places a responsibility on the leader as well as the support functions within an organisation. We will unpack the stages in detail in the next section.

 The balance of this book will look at the Onboarding model in six different stages.

**Stage 1.** Alignment – who is going to do what – and why.

**Stage 2.** Land the fish – the period between the new start signing up and their first day on the job.

**Stage 3**. The first days – when the new start arrives at work for the first time.

**Stage 4**. Getting to know my company.

**Stage 5.** Getting to know the department.

**Stage 6**. Getting to know the job – finally getting to grips with the specific role they are responsible for.

Stages 3, 4 and 5 could take place in sequence – one after another – or in parallel (all at once).

If it is your intention in reading this book to implement at some level, or improve your Onboarding process, it makes sense to start by having a high-level look at your company's Onboarding practices. Use the questionnaire on the following page to reflect on your Onboarding practices.

## An Onboarding Checklist

This is not a definitive list of Onboarding activities, but rather an Onboarding effectiveness checklist.

**On a scale of 1 to 5 please rate the following questions using the scale**
**1 – strongly disagree, 2 – mostly disagree, 3 – neutral,**
**4 – agree, 5 – strongly agree.**

| | | |
|---|---|---|
| 1. | A new start at our company has been communicated with between the employment finalisation contract and the start of work. | |
| 2. | We have invested time and effort building the new start's perception of the new company. | |
| 3. | All new starts' entry into the company have been carefully managed. | |
| 4. | All new starts are fully equipped on day one. | |
| 5. | All employee administration is completed in the first week. | |
| 6. | All new employees are able to explain the company vision and values as soon as possible. | |
| 7. | All new employees can describe the company in full by the end of the month. | |

| | |
|---|---|
| 8. All new employees know the names of all the key employees in their department. | |
| 9. All new employees can explain what each employee in their department does. | |
| 10. New employees can describe the key purpose of their new department. | |
| 11. The new employee has a clear idea what their new role is. | |
| 12. The new employee has a plan as to how and when the employee will gain the experience needed to do the job. | |
| 13. My company treats all new starts with great care. | |
| 14. My company has a comprehensive Onboarding process. | |
| 15. My company holds leaders accountable for the quality of the Onboarding process. | |

# Chapter 2

## A Comprehensive Onboarding Model

> A 5-stage Onboarding process, from signing on to company competent.

## Introduction

Chatting to the CEO of a company I provide services to he reflected: "I don't think there is enough in Onboarding to write a book about" when I told him I was writing this book. He further reflected that "in my company, we have always done this induction stuff well". As a client I did not want to argue with him, so I asked him the simple question: *"So what is the objective of the Onboarding process – making the new start feel welcome, ensuring that they are able to do the job they were employed to do as quick as possible?"*

He stopped and thought about it for a moment and then responded: *"Perhaps I am taking too narrow a view of this. We tend to bring new starts in, induct them and then get on with it."* In other words: *"Push them in the deep end?"* I asked. *"Yes, exactly,"* he replied. *"And do you think that that would be best practice."* I asked? *"While it ultimately works, perhaps not, but it works for us,"* he replied.

*"So as the new start's leader, are your responsible, and is it in your interest to get them up and running as soon as possible?"* *"Yes,"* he replied. *"Would you say that you have total control of the pace at which a new start reaches full competency?"* I responded. *"Um."* On a roll now, I pushed further: *"Are you happy with the speed of learning?"* *"No, not at all,"* he replied. *"If you put it that way, it seems to take forever, perhaps there is space for a relook."*

It is a no brainer that we need to invest in a new start, not just to save time and money, help to build a team quickly or build the confidence of the new start in their ability in the new environment, but to ensure that the new start and you, their leader, begin to build a positive work relationship.

Some time ago, my team were challenged by our MD to dramatically improve the Onboarding process of our organisation. He was not saying we were not doing a decent job, he just felt that we could do more. While we were very good at the traditional induction process, among other things, we had a rehearsed reception process – a company video, a range of standard talks and a full information pack. Employees reflected in the post-recruitment interviews that they felt somewhat underprepared, and while they were appreciative of the way we did things, they rated the process 7/10.

We were not happy about this and decided to revisit our processes. While doing a brainstorming session we finally had a profound insight. The term 'induction' was limiting our thinking. We were looking at Onboarding as a single event, an induction. We were essentially putting on an HR show, a first-day drama.

When we started looking at the outcome we desired, we started to see something different. If the outcome of the induction was just informing the new start of some policies and impressing them with the company's capacity, then we were doing great, but if the outcome was to ensure that they were able to do the job they were employed for when we recruited them, then we were far off the mark.

Unless we are involved in some form of graduate recruitment, in most cases, we spend a lot of time looking for and contracting an employee who has the broad generic capabilities to do the type of work the position requires. It is true though that unless the new employee has previously worked for us, it is impossible to appoint someone who is immediately able to fully function in our organisation. Helping an employee to move from being a competent generalist to being a skilled organisation-aligned employee is a far bigger process with a significant leadership responsibility. A responsibility which has a much wider impact on the employee and the organisation. It will require effort and focus but will, if done well, be really meaningful.

I like to ask HR people how long a full Onboarding would take, and irrespective of the position, the most common response is six months. This cannot be right for all positions:

> If you look at the Onboarding process as a time line which starts with the new start signing the employment contract, and concludes when the employee is fully competent, then the process we are discussing could be anything from a few months to a year or so.

In our brainstorming session we identified a five-component model that seemed to make sense. During a presentation of this to HR managers, they suggested that I add an alignment phase to start with – the first two components building on each other or, if you will, in sequence, and the final three in parallel. We chose some fun names just to stimulate thinking.

## Five-component Onboarding model

1. Land the Fish– the period between signing up and starting work.

2. The first days

3. Get to know the Giant – learn about the company.

4. Who is who in the Zoo – learn about the department we have joined.

5. Become company competent (lose the learner wheels) – while we may have the generic skills to perform a function, during this period we learn the specific and company-unique competencies necessary to perform the function.

Figure 1: Five Stage Onboarding Process

Each of these phases is dealt with separately in the book as a new chapter.

While potentially all five elements are possible with each appointment, we want to stress, however, that every organisation and every position filled will require a different version of these stages.

We further looked at two types of Onboarding which have very specific elements – Onboarding the "new start" and leadership Onboarding. As we worked with this it also became abundantly clear that each phase of this Onboarding process shifts dramatically based on the seniority of the position and, while for all employees the same stages exist, the level in the organisation will dramatically shift the content.

In order to develop a culture of great Onboarding it is necessary to ensure that there is a clear understanding of the roles of the HR department (if there is one), management (including Senior management), team members, technical experts and the new employees themselves. We look at this in the section called "Who does what?"

### 👁 *Let's take a quick look at the context of each phase:*

## Land the Fish

There is an uneasy period between a new start selecting to join your company, and their first day on the job. This is a significant opportunity to do something special.

## The first days

We all remember our first day in a new organisation as being extremely stressful; so much to take in and so many people to remember.

## Get to know the Giant

While we may be able to pick up some sense of who the company is that we have just hitched our wagon to, it can take years to really grasp the scope of the organisation. What is our geographic spread, who are our leaders, what are our vision and values, who are our customers, what are our products, who are the key stakeholders and where do I fit in to all of this? Depending on the size of the organisation and the seniority of the position, this stage could be a vital part of the Onboarding process.

## Who is who in the Zoo?

Who does what In this new department is a critical stage of Onboarding. Naturally, if the new start is to play a leadership role this could be the most important learning. Even if the new start is to play a role as part of a team, clarifying who does what is a critical part of the Onboarding.

## Become company competent

Without question the most critical part of the Onboarding process. It is our view that this is only mastered if you are clear on what the knowledge is that you are required to acquire. Even if we have significant past skills in a similar field, there are always areas of competency which we need to acquire. These range from simple things such as how to process purchasing orders in this company and what the position signing authority is, to complex things like operating a new piece of equipment or a unique new customer type.

***Onboarding an existing employee and Onboarding into a leadership position***

One of the most stressful and complex aspects of Onboarding is the process of taking a good employee and promoting them to a more senior position within an organisation. As the person is already a known quantity, there is an even stronger tendency to use the "Sink or Swim" approach – an approach which, we argue, is far too risky, and while it requires a lot less effort, the "sink" possibility is not one we should leave to chance..

While some would tend to think of internal Onboarding as a separate process, we recommend that this internal process is equally complex and follows, to a large degree, the same set of rules. We will look at internal Onboarding in chapter 8. We want to stress that each of the five stages in many respects refers to an internal process equal.

# Chapter 3

## How to Get Started?

## Introduction

If your organisation has never done a full five-stage Onboarding process, then it is very likely that there is some sort of expectation that the responsibility to get this up and running lies with HR. As already discussed, this is unreasonable and at least unrealistic without full active organisational commitment. If this is seen as just an HR thing, it will also mean that the leadership component of Onboarding is neglected.

Our experience is that the implementation of successful Onboarding has two major hurdles:

1. Shifting line management thinking from "This is a hassle" to "This is a leadership imperative and part of my performance deliverables."

2. Shifting line response from "This is just another fad – it too will pass" to a sustained initiative. As Onboarding does not necessarily happen all the time, it often starts with a flourish, and then peters out over time.

We suggest that some form of alignment process is necessary. How this can be achieved will depend on each organisation's size and complexity so that the ideas we are presenting are assuming medium to large organisational structures. This process is, in our experience, also easily scaled down for a smaller concern.

If Onboarding is entirely new to your organisation, then successful implementation could follow the entire famous eight stages of Kotter's change processes of "our iceberg is melting" fame. We propose putting the spotlight on just five components.[5]

## Create a need

A comprehensive Onboarding process requires significant effort and unless the organisation, to some level, recognises a need to do this, emphasising the importance of the effort could become unnecessarily difficult.

How do we create the need? Here are some suggestions:

A.  Do a survey of new employees, asking some pointed questions about their Onboarding experience. The chances are that if you don't have an Onboarding culture, it is unlikely that they will respond with a rave review.

B.  Do research into turnover stats, particularly of new and younger and/or professional employees. Also look at:

   a.  Exit interviews.
   b.  New start performance management results.

C.  Collect a few cameo stories of failed Onboarding internally.

D.  Identify an "eventful" Onboarding disaster and conduct a detailed case study on it – try to avoid isolating either an HR person or a line manager.

## Get Senior Management support

While we don't expect executive management to design the programme, it will, without question, be far easier to implement if you have achieved full endorsement. It will be challenging, or impossible, to overcome the two major hurdles "acceptance and sustenance" without senior endorsement. How to do this would need organisational finesse, but obviously the "Creating the need" components will strengthen interest and resolve.

I worked for an MD who took this very seriously. Even though we were a fairly large company, he somehow kept track of all appointments. Executive management, would be guaranteed that a question would be asked about any new starts in your department during a monthly one-on-one. "I don't know", or any other sign of uncertainty would be responded to with: "Please set up an appointment with the new start and myself." This was a very humiliating experience which quickly ensured management commitment and follow-up.

## Use a cross-functional team to brainstorm a process

It goes without saying that if you intend to prevent the crafting of an Onboarding programme from being a "still born" HR process, the value of a respected cross-functional team should not be underestimated.

I have lead a number of Onboarding "cross-functional brainstorming sessions". The six-step process really helps the brainstorming and rather than trying to squeeze out ideas, you could end up in a situation where you have to run a process of selecting a manageable number of ideas.

A really great way of doing this is to use a World Café technique to design an Onboarding process and at the same time use this as a form of management team building.

---

**The World Café**

This is a great way to use a large group of people to brainstorm or discuss something.

The World Café methodology is a great way to get input on a strategic issue from a larger group of management. While World Café can be modified to meet a wide variety of needs, we have specifically

---

designed this one as a management meeting focused on developing an Onboarding strategy.

1.  *Layout*: The idea is to create an environment which resembles, as closely as possible, a café, i.e. small round tables covered with a tablecloth or paper, coloured pens and any extras you think could improve the atmosphere. There should be about five chairs at each table. For this purpose, each table would represent an element of the Onboarding process. So, five tables divided by the size of the participant group would determine the number of participants.

2.  *Welcome and Introduction*: The host begins with a warm welcome and explains the process.

3.  *Small Group Rounds*: The first, of five twenty-minute rounds of conversation will start. Each small group, seated around a table, will begin to discuss the topic represented at their table. At the end of the discussion, each team chooses one person to stay as the "table host". This person transfers to the next team what has happened so far. The group splits up and moves to a different, new table.

4.  *Questions*: We suggest asking questions along the following lines:

    ☐   Any great ideas for the "Landing the Fish" phase?

    ☐   How do we make the first days memorable?

    ☐   What do we need new starts to know about the Giant and how will we do this?

    ☐   How do we make the "Who's who in the Zoo" phase meaningful?

    ☐   How do we make the "becoming company competent" phase really effective?

5.  *Harvest*: After the small groups have circulated through all five tables, the final group prepares a presentation on what the outcome was of their table – not just in their session, but as it had been handed on from previous teams.

6.  Good coffee and a good venue helps.

## Allocate roles

For an effective Onboarding process to work, it is really important that the roles of the different stakeholders have been spelt out.

We propose the following role allocations:

## A. Senior Management including the CEO or MD

Imagine how focused everyone would be on Onboarding if each manager of a new employee was asked to review their Onboarding process at a quarterly or, more realistically, half-yearly Onboarding review.

Does the company acknowledge that there is real value in doing a great Onboarding? If so, it stands to reason that a review of recent Onboarding could well be the part of the business systems that are regularly monitored. Is this a pipe dream in most organisations? Perhaps, but should it be? How we do Onboarding is a reflection of our organisational commitment to leadership and I can guarantee that most companies' value statements would support such an initiative.

If the company already has an executive succession planning review process, this could just be added to the agenda. If not, some simple suggestions could constitute a review:

1. Introduce the new starts and their potential.
2. Consult the review of the new starts' Onboarding survey results – see the end of the section.
3. What process did they/are you still to follow?
4. Review the action plan.
5. Estimate the timeline till fully inducted.
6. Record leadership lessons derived from the process.

## B. HR role players

Clearly there are a wide range of activities which various HR role players would need to play. Every organisation would have a different list and different allocation of responsibilities and it is our proposal that this is unpacked in detail and responsibilities allocated based on skill sets. The principle is not to allocate people who are not focused in that area, for instance, filling in payroll information should happen in the payroll department.

It is our view that the HR consultant/business partner responsible for the specific department in which the new start is placed, would need to take overall accountability for the process. If we take the position at a leadership level, the line leader must take responsibility for the process as that is not primarily an HR responsibility.

Where line leadership embrace their leadership role, the HR imperative shifts to:

"Create an environment where the line leader thrives."

Far more than policing and auditing such a process, HR's role is at least to make it easy for the line leader to do, and HR can take the administrative burden off the hands of the line leader, allowing them time to do the active parts of the process which line and HR jointly designed.

In the following chapters we will explore and propose a wide range of deliberate actions that could be implemented in order to ensure that the leader succeeds. HR's role should be to develop such tools and provide an "Onboarding-friendly environment".

## C. Line leaders

We cannot stress enough that the active components of the Onboarding process should be seen by the line leader as a real opportunity to perform as a leader as opposed to just a hassle factor distracting them from their "management" functions.

Ideally the line leader should be uncompromising about the Onboarding process, passionate about its success and proud of the results. If this is already part of the organisational culture it will be easy; if not, then building a company passion for Onboarding is perhaps where this process should start.

## D.  Mentors, coaches and buddies

Increasingly, employees are open to support roles like coaching and mentoring. There is a lot of value in appointing someone independent of the line leader to play a role in the Onboarding of a new employee. This could be good practice on one condition: that such an appointment does not replace the role of the line leader. We need to take care to ensure that the direct line leader's leadership role is not replaced by a surrogate person.

In order to ensure that the line leader is not undermined by the appointment of an internal support person, it is recommended to involve the line leader in such an appointment. It is also important that the role of the support person is clearly defined and communicated to all three parties – the new start, the line leader and the support person.

Putting the roles down in a documented agreement or contract between the parties may sound over-managed but such an agreement ensures expectation alignment.

There are three possible different roles which such a support person could fill. These roles also assist in the identification of the profile of this person.

*Let's look at these different roles:*

### Mentor:

A mentor is generally a senior person with significant company and work experience. The mentor would assist the employee to adjust to the specific work environment. A mentor would take an active interest in a new employee's progress and provide a safe place for an employee to discuss experiences and gain insight.

As opposed to a coach, a mentor's experience is embraced as a valuable contribution to the new start.

**Coach:**

There is a lot of focus these days on coaching. The essential difference between a mentor and a coach is that while a mentor willingly provides insight and advice, a coach encourages the new employee to discover their potential and guides them through a thinking process. While many models of coaching exist, and different coaches use different principles, the most common is the Grow model:

**G** = Goals – assisting the employee to set specific goals
**R** = Reality – gaining clear insight into the employee's current reality
**O** = Options – assisting the employee to identify options
**W** = Will or Way forward – encouraging the employee to take deliberate actions, and providing a level of accountability

Coaching generally requires a level of skill in coaching. It not a role that just anyone can fill well.

**Buddy:**

This is a role that is uniquely designed for Onboarding processes. A buddy is someone who is identified to support the new employee in finding their way in the organisation.

A buddy  is generally someone who is just slightly more experienced than the employee and  who the employee would not regard as an elder but rather as a friend. This buddy will show the new employee the ropes and use their personal network to help the new start integrate into the organisation. A buddy also helps the new start navigate the informal networks and company politics.

This process is particularly valuable to the new employee during the first days, and the early period of the Onboarding process.

In all three alternatives a level of confidentiality and privacy is critical. Where the support person needs to engage HR or line leadership on an issue arising from the new employee, the support person would ask permission first.

# Preparing the organisation to shift to a proper Onboarding process

Sense would strongly caution against launching an Onboarding programme as another HR programme. In order to get real traction, we would advise that implementing an Onboarding process should be approached as a change management initiative. A colleague of mine, who is the HR director of an auto component subsidiary, described the process he followed as below:

---

**How change happens**

Some years ago we lost two great new appointments within three months of their starting. This was most frustrating, because both were employees with high potential for future management positions in the technical area where we had a skills deficit and had invested considerable effort in finding a new breed of engineer.

Our MD was livid and demanded a full investigation into what had happened. While we had done exit interviews, we really did not have good information, but that which we had indicated that we had seriously failed in the integration of the new starts into the company. We had the standard company induction, but it was clear that a more comprehensive process was needed. It was at this stage that we developed the five-stage model, which we will unpack in some detail in the book. Interestingly, research shows that globally, there was a similar thinking emerging about Onboarding.

We then knew what we wanted to do, but how to do it was the real challenge. Across the organisation, the prevailing view was that induction was an HR thing and Onboarding, especially a five-stage process, was overkill.

This was much more than just introducing a new process. We clearly needed a well thought out change management process.

---

Loosely based on Kotter's 8-step change model, we did the following:[6]

**Firstly:**

We put the hard numbers to the Labour turnover we experienced: what the costs were to recruit a new employee, what the waste cost was of recruiting the two employees who had left, what the estimated opportunity cost was of their positions not being effectively filled for 10 months due to the positions effectively being vacant for so long (costs of overtime, contractors, delayed projects and the opportunity cost incurred due to a delayed project implementation.)

**Secondly:**

The costs, when looked at jointly, were really exorbitant and when presented to the Manco [Management Company], elicited a strong response. This presentation created the opportunity for some high-level, hard discussions. These rigorous debates were very important in creating a deep awareness of the challenge and what could be done. While it also placed a significant amount of finger pointing at HR, this reputational risk was important. Ultimately, when leadership accountability is on the table, the HR role starts to align correctly. I had primed the MD as to what was at stake and he asked me: "So, if we really have to shake this up, what do you propose?"

**Thirdly:**

His question opened up the opportunity to present the five-stage model and, in particular, the roles outlined above. I did not present it immediately, but agreed to return with a proposal the following week.

When I did the presentation, as expected, this elicited some push back: "This is overkill, we have other things that are important, HR is pushing its responsibility on to us ...". We then held an honest discussion about role clarification, starting with the question, "So who is ultimately responsible for the Employee?" This is a crucial question and quickly sorts out the real issues that are in the leadership space.

When we looked at Onboarding as "the first step of the leadership journey", we began to shift thinking about Onboarding as an induction process to Onboarding as a Culture Change initiative and this made all the difference. (In Simon Sinek's famous TED talk he explains how, when the Why becomes clear to us, the What and the How follow – if we can find the deeper purpose in a process we make a huge difference.)[7]

We ended a very dynamic Manco session with clear roles, much like those described above. HR's role was not completed; we now needed to create the range of tools necessary to deliver on the "why" we had created.

**Fourthly**:

Having opened the door, the HR department needed to quickly return with a wide range of tools which would turn this process into a real live implementation. It was important that this was done quickly as our experience was that if you do not capitalise on such an opportunity, the organisation will soon find a new focus area and nothing will have changed.

The activities we implemented included:

- leader training in Onboarding as a leadership moment,

- an Onboarding policy,

- an Onboarding off-the-shelf IT programme,

- the training and alignment of the entire HR team in the process and philosophy of Onboarding – the why,

- the addition of Onboarding as an element of the annual performance review and

- a range of other actions which are all highlighted, either in this chapter, or in the rest of this book.

**Fifthly**:

Having successfully implemented an Onboarding process, the final step was to ensure that this new process had longevity. In our company we liked to measure stuff, even the soft stuff. Reviewing the effectiveness of the Onboarding process was then added to the Manco agenda and twice a year we reviewed:

- Employee turnover.

- Retention of new starts.

- New start Onboarding satisfaction index.

- Time to full competency per new start.

We sincerely hope that by now, Onboarding is seen in a different light to the "old school" induction programme.

*Table 1: Checklist to test the shift in thinking*

| Question | Level of agreement<br>1 - Strongly disagree<br>2 - Disagree<br>3 - Agree<br>4 - Strongly agree |
|---|---|
| Onboarding is a complex process which will require significant coordination. | |
| Developing an Onboarding process should be coordinated by HR, but with the practical involvement of line management. | |
| Executive leadership support for the Onboarding process is a critical success factor. | |
| Ultimately, the line manager is responsible to ensure that their own new start is effectively Onboarded. | |
| An employee is only Onboarded when the new start is completely integrated into the team. | |
| An employee is only Onboarded when the new start is competent in the organisational skill set they were recruited for. | |

# Chapter 4

## Land the Fish

> **Ensuring that a newly recruited employee is prepared for their introduction into a new organisation.**

## Introduction

I have spent many hours in a small boat on the Bushman's River hoping to land the elusive Spotted Grunter or White Steenbras. The greatest rush is the feeling of electricity when a big one strikes. When the rod bends you just know that all the hours spent on the bank waiting, all the bait-ups and casts and your patience were worth it.

I know that there are fishermen who love the business of fishing more than catching, but I am not one of them. I love the thrill of a big strike and getting the perfect fish on the line, but from experience I know that this is only the beginning. You only get bragging rights when the fish is in the boat. I know only too well that there is a big difference between hooking a fish and landing one. A lot can go wrong between the thrill of the strike and landing the fish.

While this is perhaps not the best analogy when it comes to appointing talent, a signed contract is, sadly, just a piece of paper. Unless your new start is unemployed, it is unlikely that he/she will start immediately. A month's notice is standard and for senior positions, and two or three months is a possibility. A lot can happen during this time period. It is almost certain that if you have really hooked a "Grunter", a great talent, the current employer would surely have put up a fight. Why would you expect a RECRUIT, who has only met you a few times during the stressful interview process, to be more loyal to you than an employer of a number of years? If working for the past employer was a good experience, you will have a fight on your hands. A fight you probably know little about.

I have experienced new recruits turning down your offer a day before they are expected to start. While this is very frustrating and while you could easily respond that "with an attitude like that it was probably for the best", the reality is that this is an extremely expensive exercise. It probably costs hours of time during the recruitment process which will need to be revitalised, but even worse, it will now cost real time. The larger challenge is that the position could remain unfilled for five to six months.

We all know what this could mean. You can just hear the financial manager saying, "We have operated so long without someone. Do we really need to appoint?"

Besides the landing fish objective, there is a further strong motivator to be deliberate and organised during the pre-first day "land the fish" phase.

Let's go back to the five major drivers of an Onboarding process and then look at the obvious practical things that we could consider doing in this first phase to enhance them.

## Speed and cost

The best-case scenario is that a vacancy is filled within two to three months, depending on the notice period. In the case of a last-minute withdrawal, the company could be without a suitable candidate to fill the position for five to six months. This can be extremely frustrating and, depending on the position, could result in loss of revenue or the overworking of current employees and the risk of further resignations.

So, what to do? Well, there are no guarantees in this process, but we are able to improve the chances of avoiding a last-minute turndown by:

- Building trust with the new start.
- Helping them to become confident.

- Building enthusiasm for the new position.

- Dealing with any concerns the new start may have.

This sounds very "touchy feely" but it is not. It's just wise leadership – not leaving anything to chance. How to do this? Some ideas are:

- A weekly check noted in the diary so that we don't forget to follow up with the new starts due to the complexity of the day-to-day quest to meet targets.

- An offsite coffee date.

- An invitation to join a department activity like a team-building or a training programme.

## Employee value proposition and building the psychological contract with your new employee

Your new employee is a very powerful influencer of marketplace opinion about your company. At this early stage of the employment relationship, small gestures will mean a great deal. Every time the new start has contact with the new company the bond strengthens as well as the perception that joining this company was a great decision. I have heard many different creative stories of companies doing things – small things that will be long remembered.

I know of a fast-moving consumer goods company that sends their new starts a product hamper a week after "sign on". Imagine signing on at your new company and a week later you receive a complementary case of soft drink or personal grooming products!

A middle-management employee received a letter from the CEO of her new company welcoming her and offering any assistance she may need to settle in. This letter alone persuaded her to turn down a lucrative counter-offer from her current company to stay, based on the logic that if the CEO could take the time to do this, the new company was likely to be far more "human" than the existing one.

A week after joining a new company as the senior executive, I was contacted by the purchasing executive, a new colleague, who asked for my sizes so that he could order my personalised corporate clothing set.

This would have been cool if it was done for all employees as a matter of course. It would have many benefits to the so-called contract, as well as just alleviating the challenge of what to wear on the first day.

This little act of thoughtfulness could be extended to choices like:

- Which company cell phone would you like us to order and let's do a sim swap before you start?
- Which PC option do you prefer?
- Which medical aid option?
- Which picture in your office?
- What would you like for lunch on your first day?
- Send the new start a copy of the company newsletter, or the annual report.
- Give the new start a flash drive with company data on it.

To take this to the next level, we could set up a meeting with the company's medical aid and insured benefits consultant. During such a meeting the consultant would explain the options to the new start and advise on the best package.

These are more practical things we could close off with which would help the new employee through the first day's stress and change.

## Company induction information

Some years back we developed a smart induction video, at some expense, for the first-day induction. Thinking back on it now, I think it would have been far more meaningful if we had sent it out during the "landing the fish" phase. This video included:

- A message from the CEO.

- An explanation about the company values and vision.

- Our best behaviours (like a code of ethics).

- The senior organogram with a brief interview with each senior executive.

- A fun role play about the company safety rules.

- Some product knowledge.

## Online Onboarding systems

I have seen some IT companies advertising "Onboarding best practice software". Essentially this means that the new start's administration is efficiently managed through a software package and, while "this could be costly to set up", it does sound smart. However, this is not a replacement for the "land the fish" phase of this process. This is not about admin; admin is the given. This is about engagement and building a trust relationship.

While a smart IT system can help a lot and make the Onboarding process as pain free as possible, it may never replace the "human dynamic".

---

**A practical caution**

It is possible to try to persuade your new start to breach employment notice periods, as there is very little legal recourse if an employee breaches contracted notice. It is our strong recommendation that you do not consider this. Among the persuasive arguments against such a breach are:

1. Do you really want to start an employment relationship with an ethical issue?

2. If you do not hold another employer's notice period as sacred, why would you expect your employees to hold yours in any esteem?

3. This is a strong symbol to all employers about loyalty and integrity.

---

## Building a high-performance team

So, how can we use the "landing the fish" period to build a team and quickly integrate the new start into the team? There would seem to be two areas of opportunity:

1.  To build the image of the new start in the eyes of the team.

2.  To quickly build relationships between the team and the new start.

---

**Two Experiences of Onboarding:**

*Put yourself in the employee's shoes. Imagine that you have just been appointed into a dream job. While you are happy in your current position and company, as you have grown up with the current employer, they have seemed reluctant to recognise your promotional potential. Now this new employer has offered you the position you dreamed of and you have tendered your resignation and will leave the employer you know, to take up the new position in a month in a scary, totally new, environment.*

**Scenario 1**

Your recruitment agent has processed all the contract stuff and you are now in that uncomfortable "I am leaving" phase. Your current employer has developed a deep regret for not looking after you better. You have been called into the Director's office and he has gently put a lot of pressure on you: "Don't give me an answer now but these are the plans we have for you." He has outlined a development plan, a mentorship programme, a business school opportunity and the opportunity to visit overseas facilities. They will also meet your current new employer's offer and package. You wake up in the middle of the night and battle to sleep. You really can't decide what to do. Start fresh as a new expert employee in an unknown environment or stay in you comfort zone? The closer it comes to the end of the month, the more difficult you find it to say no to your Director. While he has placed no pressure on you, you know he expects a positive response, and you feel a high level of loyalty.

---

**Scenario 2**

While the scenario is the same from your existing employer's point of view, your new employer has been a revelation.

On the day after you signed up, you had received a letter from their MD welcoming you to the new company and outlining the exciting new directions the company is exploring. You were given in-house online access to the company's dynamic product training videos. Every week your new company's manager calls and asks you how you are doing and if there is anything she can do to help? In the second week you were invited to after-work drinks with the team and felt very welcome, pleasantly surprised by how cool your future work colleagues are.

Last week you were sent a choice list asking you for your laptop and cell phone preferences, as well as your shoe and shirt sizes in preparation for ordering you a full set of shirts and safety shoes for your first day.

You already feel part of the team and you have not yet started. Your diary for the first weeks arrived yesterday, sent by the HR Executive. Just when you started to stress about how you would adapt to the new environment, they have put together a detailed plan which will quickly let you catch up.

While you are pleased about the sudden recognition you are now receiving from the management of your current employer, your new employer is in a different league to your existing employer when it comes to valuing employees and being proactive and organised.

My own poor experience of joining a new management team had a lot to do with "first days". The MD had asked me to negotiate a few days' orientation with the company before I officially started. As I was locating to a new city, far away from my home of many years, the entire experience of those weeks was telling.

The intent of having me come up and spend time in the company before I started formally – I had a three-month notice period – was a good one. However, the experience left me with some real concerns about my decision to change employers. The reason for my "concern" was more to do with the social dynamic than what I encountered on site.

While I respect the fact that people have families and social time is of high value, wondering around a new city by yourself, getting lost in traffic, not knowing where to set up house and eating alone night after night, was a lost opportunity for me. My entry into the new company could have been very different if there had been some level of interest in settling me down on the part of my new peers. If I had started on day one with a friendly face and someone with whom I had some common interest, even if it was just the knowledge of their favourite restaurant, it would have made a huge difference.

Research shows that trust is key to a high-performing work team. Patrick Lencioni, in his famous book on why teams fail, records that a lack of trust is the first and most common reason teams are unable to perform.[8]

However, as they say, trust is earned. The question is how? The answer is obvious; I will only start really trusting you when I get to know you. Although it is most common to introduce a new team member to the team on day one, we would suggest letting the new start spend some time with your team prior to that day for real reasons of good value:

- It quickly neutralises the "rumour" effect.
- It means that the first day will be much easier on both your existing team and the new member.
- When people meet on a human level before they encounter the challenges of the "work environment", they find it much easier to find commonality and points where they naturally connect.

While each company culture is different and each circumstance determined by the people involved, a team brainstorming could generate some ideas as to how to do this. But in this space Authenticity is important. This will work very differently depending on levels of seniority, function and age group. Here are some ideas for a new member of an executive team:

Someone calling in and saying, "Hi Joe, I'm your new colleague in finance. We have a meeting in your town and I wondered if you would like to get together for a glass of wine and chat about the inside track."

1. **A new graduate:**

   The team leader calling up and inviting you: "The team (your new team) are celebrating Jane's promotion tomorrow evening at the Bru Bar. Come and meet the crew."

   "Why don't you join our 'WhatsApp' group? It is purely a social group."

2. **A new team member joining a professional team:**

   "We meet every Friday for a drink (or stock cars), we have a social rugby team and see you are a prop. Heard on the grapevine that you have a 12 handicap. Why don't you join the guys for a 4-ball?"

3. **A new manager:**

   "Hi Joe, I hear you have taken up the new position as logistics manager. I am the purchasing manager and I know that we will be working closely together. I am looking forward to having you on board. Please join me and the warehouse manager after work at the plant and we will show you around."

## Preparing for day one

It goes without saying that the prep work to make day one "cook" needs to be done well in advance. All the soft stuff we have discussed thus far will amount to nothing if we don't get the basics correct on day one.

My interviews with employees about first days, across organisations, show that, so often, this process which could be so easy, is a disaster.

As some of the items, such as order in a PC, may take some time, we propose that this part of the process is, to a large degree, automated. In other words, as soon as a new start has accepted and signed the employment contract, the day one preparation process is initiated. An effective day one preparation should be:

1.  Seamless.

2.  Automated.

3.  Absolutely reliable.

4.  With clear accountabilities.

5.  Clear deadlines – before; not on start.

As we are all busy, the more automated this could be made, the better. A very low-cost system we used for years with limited chance of failure, but assuming that the new start would need at least one month's notice before starting, was as follows:

1.  We developed a standard checklist of requirements for all employee new starts. This list had a general section for all and another for the job and/or level-specific requirements (see example in Appendix 3)

2.  Every vacancy approved was controlled as soon as a position was approved by the HR administrator who was a Supervisor/Manager. We did this for several reporting reasons, including managing turnaround time, salary planning, headcount management and head office reporting.

3.  As soon as an appointment was made, the administrator would record acceptance and generate a checklist automatically, based on the position. This checklist had a standard set of people who were designated specific actions; i.e. order PC, order safety shoes etc...

4.   All requirements for the new start were registered per position; i.e. office or laptop was a position allocation as per choice. In each case the responsible department would confirm check sheet acceptance and an expected time of achievement.

5.  The administrator would automatically diarise a follow-up date.

6.  The line manager responsible for the new start would receive a weekly report on progress.

A bit over the top, perhaps, but better that than dropping the ball.

# Conclusion

As a final thought, it is appropriate to reflect again on the "why". When Onboarding is seen as a strategic imperative, the "why" becomes clearer.

The following five questions will help us to check the effectiveness of each step of the five-stage Onboarding process and so we will repeat them for each new context.

The "land the fish" phase is probably the area with the most potential, but probably the phase on which we place the least focus. In this section we hope that you have gained an insight into what is possible. While we would propose that your organisation develop a process you own, you may want to use the items on the checklist, as idea starters, at the end of the section.

In the next chapter we are going to look at, perhaps, the one phase that most organisations get right, at least to some extent. It will be evident that what we need to do on the "first day" phase will be influenced by what has already been achieved while landing the fish.

---

**?** Key "why" questions for the "land the fish."

1.  **Speed**: By the time the new employee started, had he/she already gained a lot of the basic information necessary to get started?

2.  **Employee value proposition**: When the new start talks about us (the new company), would we be proud of what he/she says?

3.  **Team relations**: Are the members of the team that the new start will join, excited about working with their new colleague? Are they already committed to help onboard him/her?

4.  **Psychological contract**: To what extent has the new employee shifted his/her loyalty and commitment to the new company?

5.  **Leadership imperative:** Has the leader already built some degree of a trust-based relationship with the new start?

---

**How about a note on how to handle first days?**

Dear "Jenny"

We are thrilled that you will be joining our team on May first. Our HR team have put together a brief list of ideas which will help you to have a great First Day. These are just ideas we have collected over the years which you may find useful:

What to wear? Our general dress code is semi-formal. Men do not wear ties or jackets. Women dress office style and we are all a bit more relaxed on Fridays. Jeans and Golf shirts are common.

There will be five people all starting on the first.

Jane – Finance
Xolile – Quality
Jack – Engineering
Allen – a graduate from head office; and yourself.

Please meet in the foyer at 8am, we will gather there and then work together for the morning.

You will be joining your manager at lunch time (food will be provided – please ensure that we are advised if you have any special requirements).

The agenda for the day will be:

- ◊ Welcome (all management)
- ◊ Address by the CEO
- ◊ A brief Health and Safety video.
- ◊ Walk through the main building
- ◊ Why we love our products – tasting and experience.
- ◊ Lunch with your manager
- ◊ Meet the team
- ◊ Basic admin wrap-up.
- ◊ Day one debrief.
- ◊ End day one....

---

These are some ideas about preparing for the first day;

- Get a good night's sleep – there is nothing to worry about.

- Select what you will wear the next day.

- Make sure you know the way to work and what the traffic will be like.

- Prepare an "elevator pitch" – a quick, interesting introduction of yourself. You will be introducing yourself often.

- Go to our website and just look through to overall comments.

- Have a light breakfast.

- Attached is the organogram of your new department. We suggest you read through the names a few times so that you will start remembering them ASAP.

Looking forward to getting to know you.

Regards
Laura

# Chapter 5

## The First Days

*Ensuring that an employee's first days leave a positive first impression.*

## Introduction

For a long time, in my department, one of the stars of my first day induction programme was Henk. He was responsible for security in our company and as our products were high-value small items, we invested a lot of time in protecting the finished product. Henk loved what he did and was very passionate about it. There was nothing he enjoyed more than inducting new employees. He also always offered to do the Health and Safety talk that we had to do for our quality system.

As Henk was a great communicator and everything seemed to be going well, I made the fatal mistake of not checking up. When Henk started insisting that he needed more time for his section of induction (he already had an hour), I decided it was time to check it out.

Henk started off well, building rapport and telling the new employees about how long he had worked in the company and how great a place this company was to work in. But then came the security stuff. Henk had seen it as his job to scare the new employees with the consequences of taking even one product out of the plant, even if by accident. I started to wonder why people had lasted more than one day! He told dramatic stories of how they had trapped and caught dishonest employees, including a famous incident involving a spy camera. Then came Health and Safety. Henk jumped into to this topic as if he were personally responsible for saving the lives of every new start. He had decided that the best way to do this was to build on the scare tactic that he was now comfortable with.

To my horror, he began to show the fear-stricken new starts, who were already subconsciously feeling guilty about stuff they had never thought of stealing, the consequences of not following Health and Safety rules. He had collected a series of pictures – real-life pictures – of the consequences of not wearing eye protection, when using a lathe, or not wearing safety shoes in the factory.

My heart sank. Henk was so well intentioned, but so off the mark. After the session I asked some employees, who had recently joined the company, including a very senior member of the finance department, if they had the same experience, which they had. "Why did you not say something?" I asked the senior member. She replied: "I did not have the heart, he was so passionate."

## What can we do on the first day to create a lasting impression?

## It makes sense to be strategic about why we do what we do, and how.

## Opening thoughts

Most companies I have spoken to agree that, to some degree, they get this phase right. While, of course, this is very possible, we would like to invite you to take a fresh look at this phase. Perhaps you will gain new insight and value.

As with all processes we design, if we start by clearly understanding the outcomes (the why) first, our design has a reasonable chance of being something exceptional.

The problem with this phase in larger organisations is determining whose objectives (whose "why") take presidency in this phase:

1.  *HR Administration, who need to get everything on the system ASAP so that they can organise benefits as well as be ready for the first pay run.*
2.  *Health and Safety, who are at risk until the new start has been safely inducted, and they can now say an accident is the employee's fault.*
3.  *IT, who are responsible for getting the employee online, trained, and safely loaded onto their precious business management system.*
4.  *ISO accredited organisations, which require "tick-box proof" that the new employee has been job-inducted.*
5.  *Line leaders, needing to get the employee up and running.*
6.  *The training department, who have training targets to meet.*

We would like to suggest that all the above are relevant and will have to be catered for in the process. But this is not the "why" of the first day. If we focus on any of the above, we will most likely be developing little more than a tick-box exercise, or unleashing a Henk onto our new starts. Why? Because:

***The new employee (irrespective of age or experience) is guaranteed to be experiencing a significant level of stress and bewilderment at this stage and, as a result, is unlikely to learn or retain much.***

So what can we use the first day for when considering the five Onboarding imperatives?

Speed and
cost

Employee value
proposition

The psychological
contract

Onboarding
Drivers

Building a
team

The leadership
moment

## Speed and costs

As we know, the core idea of this driver is that the sooner we get the new start up and running, the less the Onboarding process costs us. During this phase the speed and cost of getting the start-up stuff out of the way are paramount.

It would be better if all the necessary admin of Onboarding is already covered at this point. We are so good at booking and doing stuff online these days. My wife arranged our entire three-week trip to Spain this year without ever needing to leave her lounge. So, why should we not be completing the basic HR administration of Onboarding in the same way, prior to the employee starting? It just requires that we get organised. I recently worked with an HR team who had identified that their Onboarding documentation amounted to some 38 pages, mostly made up of endless duplication. It only took an afternoon's brainstorming to cut it down to three pages.

Best practice I have seen involves a very smart app which gives the new start access to the full administration package on an online mobile. This app also includes company information, PR materials and user-friendly company policies.

So yes, a little admin – but just a little.

## Psychological contract and, therefore, the employee value proposition

These are perhaps the two most important "why's" in this phase of Onboarding. By the end of the first day our new start should be convinced that their decision to join us was a great one. How can we achieve this?

I think the first basic principle for first days should be to keep it light on content and admin and high on relationships.

Yes, we need to do some Health and Safety stuff for the ISO requirements, so let us make sure that we do this in such a way that the new start is not bored to death, or overwhelmed by data. How about a quick video or a pamphlet with the "8 things you should know about safety" to meet the requirements? It is all that is necessary. And from an Admin perspective? What do we need to do, that is so urgent, that it must be done on the first day and has not already been done?

On the other hand, making the new start really feel welcome is probably where the greatest energy should be spent when designing a good programme.

When I present on this topic, I play a memory game using faces which I flash up on a screen for varied intervals, as a competition. The idea is to show the audience how little we are able to retain and this is especially true when we are under pressure. Some people are very good at recalling names, but others, like myself, find this to be a real challenge.

When the objective is to assist the new employee to develop relationships quickly, it would be advisable to find ways to help them do this. In most cases we walk new employees through what to them, at this stage, is a maze of passageways, introducing them to endless different, friendly people. Is this useful? Well, perhaps in the absence of any other solution, it is fine.

By now the idea of being "deliberate" about Onboarding has been established. In this case, introducing the new start to new people on the first day should be equally deliberate.

So, how to do this well? Here are some examples of deliberate name retention:

- How about giving the new start an organogram with a picture of each person the new start needs to get to know and asking them to tick each one as they are introduced.

- When I studied art at school, I had to learn to recognise artists on sight. This was done by flashing pictures on a screen and having to remember who the artist or the title of the painting was. This worked amazingly well, and I can still remember much of it – some 30 years later! In today's world this could easily be done on a cell phone.

- I have a colleague who prided himself on being able to redraw the organograms of the global senior management team. It never seemed important to me, but this ability allowed him to position himself politically.

- Arrange a meeting with the mentor or buddy and ask them, in a non-threatening way to establish if the recruit has remembered the names of key associates. It may be difficult for the new recruit to find out themselves if they are not sure.

More than just remembering names, but spending quality time with a few important people, will leave a far stronger impression than an endless list of people.

So, who should they get to know during the first days? Here are a few suggestions:

1.  The group you start with – it is amazing how starting on the same day can build a bond between employees, irrespective of their positions.

2.  Getting to know your new boss and your boss's boss.

3.  The new team. Whether the new start is a member of a new team or an existing team, or even, importantly, the leader of a team, getting to know the team quickly is a crucial part of this process.

4.  Who's who in the zoo – there are people who will directly impact on the new start's functioning. Each person would have a different list.

## Building the team

In many organisations the new start does not meet their future work colleagues at all. At best, the new start gets to meet the team quickly, in a brief introduction. There is a potential to shift this a little. Some ideas include:

1.  We could ask one of the team members to partner the new start and lead them through the process.

2.  We could have a lunch with the team.

3.  We could ask the members of the team to do some of the induction presentations themselves.

4.  We could set up a "speed dating session" with the team – five minutes per team member. I have heard of two different millennial organisations (organisations lead by young millennial leaders).

# The leadership moment

When leaders approach the first days of an employee as a "leadership moment", the leader will view the first days in a very different way to the manager, who views the first days as a process which needs to be concluded.

I think this is best Illustrated by Xolile's story.

---

### Xolile's first day, a leadership moment

This was illustrated by a young manager, Xolile, who told me about his experience when he started an admin position at a small town depot branch of a large company. He arrived without any real instructions and dressed in his "Sunday best" for his first day. The team was friendly enough. I am told that the leadership team were meeting with the regional manager and were not in the office.

The team all looked great, all dressed in company shirts and matching jeans. They placed him in front of a PC and logged him on to the formal company induction programme. This programme was technically smart, but dull as heck. It took him through the history of the company, it's structure, some Health and Safety stuff and a summary of all the policies and procedures. Xolile reflected: 'I was beginning to feel like I was being processed just like the products that the company sold.' Definitely a management process which lacked leadership.

This was all to change. The management meeting ended and the senior team, including my future new manager, James, returned to the office. They greeted Xolile and went on with their business. About three hours later the regional manager arrives. He walks through the offices greeting all the people working there. He knows each by name and seems to have a point of contact with them. When he gets to Xolile's desk, where Xolile was still wading through company policies, he smiles and says: 'I don't know you. I am Herman, but everybody calls me Harry. So, you must be the new guy they told me about.'

Then Harry does the unthinkable. He asks: 'Why are you wearing these formal clothes? Give me a second, you are about the same size as me, I have a spare shirt in the car, give me a moment.' Harry arrives moments later and gives Xolile a shirt. 'Slip this on and then let's go for lunch.'

He calls James. 'Hey James! That report can wait; we have a new colleague here and we need to get to know him.' They spend the next two hours chatting at the coffee shop around the corner that the company uses. Harry really took time to ask him about his life, his family and how they were coping with the relocation and offered to help with school challenges Xolile was experiencing. Xolile reflected that: 'Every time James tried to angle the discussion about work, Harry would direct the conversation back to getting to know me.'

---

Xolile said to me that James never really built any type of relationship with him, but Harry would drop him a line every now and then, and when he visited the region he would always make sure that he caught up with him and he would always ask about his children's school. When he took up the position he now has as their competitor, the regional manager, he was fine with leaving James, but leaving Harry was different. He still considers him to be the best leader he has experienced in his career and, even though they are competitors, Harry still takes the time to keep in contact with him. Finally Xolile reflected: 'I don't think this was something special, Harry does this with everyone.'

As we discussed in in a previous section, modern thinking about leadership is very clear. Leadership starts with the relationship. If you are uncomfortable with building relationships with your subordinates, you are probably not leading, you are managing. How will an employee learn to trust you if you are distant and personally disinterested? We maintain that it would be exceptionally difficult. We also maintain that leaders who are not trusted will also not have the ability to exert influence without using positional power.

First days are unique opportunities to build that leadership relationship for a number of reasons:

- First days are unique in that they are once-off occurrences. As a result, they will be remembered and will have the ability to leave a lasting impression.
- If a leader uses the first days effectively to build the relationship, the leadership relationship will be founded from the outset. This is very powerful over the long term.
- First days are not cluttered with work issues and are purely about getting to know each other.
- When the leader makes the new employee's first day a priority, it sends a very strong message to the rest of the team; about the importance of the new employee and the responsibility of the rest of the team to build and support the new start.

The real issue here is, does the leader take a real active interest in the new start and is he authentically interested? if so, we are really

Onboarding, as opposed to leaving induction to some HR administrative system.

---

**?** **Key "why" questions which will confirm the effectiveness of the "the first days".**

1. **Speed**: Were the first days a heavy admin, dull experience? But also, importantly, have we now cleared away any admin necessary? Are all the basic workplace arrangements in place (office, phone, email, pc, company vehicle issued and the basic security accesses established)?

2. **Employee value proposition**: Having been through the first days, has the new start been blown away by how organised, professional and progressive the new organisation is?

3. **Team relations**: Does the new start know all the names of the new team members and is the new start able to begin a conversation with each of them? Have the team got to know the new start and begun the process of building the new start into the team?

4. **Psychological contract**: Does the new team member feel welcome and that they are an important part of the new company?

5. **Leadership imperative:** At the end of the first days the new start will have begun to develop a perception about their new leader. What is that perception and is it in line with the leader's "personal leadership brand," the intentional brand of leadership they are building?

---

**Here are 21 things you should do on the first day of your new job (modified from Jacquelyn Smith[9])**

1. Ask yourself: What don't I know that is important to know at this stage? Prepare and ask questions.

2. Be on time – you do not need the stress of being late on the first day. Watch out for the traffic which can often be very different early in the morning.

3. Prepare an elevator pitch. You will need this, so planning a great story is important.

4. Choose your friends carefully. Be sure to connect with those who are building careers vs those who are stagnant.

5. Bring your A game – sleep well, plan wardrobe etc.

6. Smile.

7. When unsure about the dress code – ask – but rather over than under.

8. Do the handshake thing and make eye contact.

9. Talk to everybody. You want to understand the organisation from every angle.

10. Make a friend.

11. Don't try too hard. Keep your experience and ideas to yourself for now. Listen.

12. Don't turn down lunch. Any social setting is an opportunity to connect.

13. Listen and observe.

14. Project positivity and enthusiasm.

15. Listen for the "single most important thing" the company needs from you now!!

16. You need to be 100% present at work, especially on the first day. Leave your cell phone in your locker.

17. Tell me more – do I understand this correctly? Show interest in everyone and the company.

18. Is your body language an issue? Pay attention.

19. Building a relationship with the boss is the thing that will help you the most. Take careful note of the core messages coming from this side.

20. Be yourself.

21. Leave with a good attitude.

# Chapter 6

## Getting to know the Giant

> *Assisting the new employee to get to know their employer's entire business.*

## Introduction

It is our suggestion that the next three phases develop simultaneously: "getting to know the Giant", "who is who in the Zoo" and "becoming company competent". It is not necessary that they happen in sequence, but clearly, learning to master the technical elements required in the last section could most often take the longest.

What do we mean by "getting to know the Giant"? We chose this title to illustrate the organisational size and complexity dimensions of the organisation, which the new employee needs to grasp in order to begin to add real value.

Imagine you encountered a real giant – as in "Jack and the bean stalk" type of giant. You are so small in comparison that if you first encountered the giant's toe, the toe would tower over you. How do you get to understand what you are dealing with? Is this a friendly giant or a two-headed monster? Well, until someone tells you, it is unlikely that you will be able to guess.

Even an internet search tells you very little and certainly will not give you a real sense of the culture, history, ethics or geographic structure of the organisation.

Well, you could argue that it is not important for the new start to grasp all this stuff. While for the most menial of jobs, this could be valid to some degree, we think that this is very old-fashioned thinking. Our world has changed dramatically in terms of interconnectedness. Employees can build connections across even the largest of global organisations and it is in this very connectiveness that the strength of an organisation is optimised.

These are some examples:

- I have recently come across an international pharmaceutical organisation that has established an international "pen pals" type of network encouraging employees across the group to connect and share experiences. They report that the outcome of this activity has been remarkable.

- At a different organisation they have established a global network of women in leadership.

- I know that in many auto plants new employees will spend at least a week working on the production line, irrespective of whether they are admin employees or the new sales director.

- I have seen new starts take part in cross-functional projects.

- I have seen production people conducting trade visits and salespeople spending time on the production shop floor.

- I know of a manufacturing director who spent a day working in the medical department, as well as an evening in the security offices.

- It is not uncommon for senior employees to spend time overseas in the head office of the Giant, if multinational, but there are companies who invest fortunes in giving employees, at various levels, such an experience.

- I know of a company that has the history of the company illustrated as a flow diagram and any new start is expected to be able to tell the story to visitors.

- I have developed self-study product guides, using layman's terms, which each new start needs to go through, using scripts, videos and online questionnaires to confirm learning.

Some of my personal experiences in "getting to know the Giant" stand out:

First, as a new graduate in a remarkably progressive company at the time, the CEO of the organisation spent two days with the graduates, in a very informal and status-free environment, sharing with them his personal story of how he had progressed in the company, teaching them about the company, challenging them to question assumptions. Who better to explain the company's visions and values! Advice he gave was: "At...... we have many managers; find a good one and work hard for him. If you push him/her up the ladder, he/she will take you with them." I can still clearly remember this experience many years later.

The second "getting to know the Giant" experience went differently. I was already questioning the decision to join a specific company, as I felt that there was an ethical mismatch between them and myself. Five months after joining, I visited the global head office. What I discovered during a week at the head office not only confirmed my fears, but I could see clearly where the mismatch had its origins. On my return my wife and I began to develop an exit strategy. In my case this discovery was both in my, and the company's best interest.

Of course, "getting to know the Giant" will differ from organisation to organisation. How things are done, and to what level of complexity, would be determined by two things:

- ▪ by each organisation size locally and internationally and
- ▪ the nature of the position the new start fills.

While each company is different, following are some possible "getting to know the Giant" themes:

*Table 2: Getting to know the Giant themes*

|    | Ideas | Relevant | Irrelevant |
|----|-------|----------|------------|
| 1  | The what and why of our values | | |
| 2  | How the product is manufactured/ developed | | |
| 3  | Who the key role players are | | |
| 4  | Key challenges/opportunities | | |
| 5  | Key players | | |
| 6  | Education and training opportunities | | |
| 7  | Competitors and market dynamics | | |
| 8  | Shareholding structures | | |
| 9  | Company principles on principle issues e.g. discrimination, harassment, race, religion | | |
| 10 | The company calendar – what happens when | | |
| 11 | The goals/vision | | |
| 12 | The geographic nature of the business | | |
| 13 | Career pathing | | |
| 14 | History of the company | | |
| 15 | Future strategies and project plans | | |
| 16 | Emerging technologies | | |
| 17 | Market dynamics | | |
| 18 | Key customers | | |

| | Ideas | Relevant | Irrelevant |
|---|---|---|---|
| 19 | Governing/quality managing systems and entities | | |
| 20 | The global organogram | | |
| 21 | Partner companies | | |
| 22 | Union/management dynamics and agreements | | |
| 23 | Company annual report and how to read it | | |
| 24 | The share price and what it means | | |
| 25 | Company security systems | | |
| 26 | Overview of the IT infrastructure | | |
| 27 | The company suggestion schemes/ continuous improvement process/ideas management | | |
| 28 | Company training and education policies and how to access these | | |
| 29 | The start to end production and sales process | | |
| 30 | The organisation's quality management systems | | |
| 31 | The company's authorisations manual. Who can sign off what. | | |
| 32 | The company budgeting process and timing | | |
| 33 | The industry history | | |

| | Ideas | Relevant | Irrelevant |
|---|---|---|---|
| 34 | The previous year's financial and key performance indicators | | |
| 35 | Colleagues who do the same work as you but in different plants, countries, sister organisations. | | |
| 36 | The CEO's vision of the future | | |
| 37 | Company evacuation procedure | | |
| 38 | Company art and logo templates and rules | | |
| 39 | Company confidentiality policy | | |

**?** Key "why" questions which will confirm the effectiveness of "Getting to know the Giant."

**Speed and cost**: Does the new start have sufficient insight into the company as a whole and a working insight into the organisation as to how their specific role fits into the wider organisation? Practically, can the new start draw/describe how the company fits together?

1. **Employee value proposition**: Having "got to know the Giant", what is the impression of the new start? Is the new start "a company person"?
2. **Team relations**: Does the new start have relationships with the key role players in their scope of impact across the organisation? This is easily achieved in a single geographic location, not so in a larger organisation.
3. **Psychological contract**: Does the new team member fit in with the values of the company they joined?
4. **Leadership imperative:** How would the new start rate their leader's commitment to their Giant lessons? From irrelevant: "Get on with the job" to "I am committed to your gaining a big-picture view of the company quickly."

# Chapter 7

## Who is Who in the Zoo?

> Assisting the new employee to become part of the team.

## Introduction

We use this title "who is who in the zoo" to describe the process of getting to know the colleagues who have a direct impact on the new start's position. This part of the Onboarding process is important not just for the new start but for the entire team or department. This is also often the aspect that we do not do or pay limited attention to. During this phase, we focus on three elements:

1. Developing a relationship with the different role players.

2. Getting a reasonable understanding of what each of their positions entails.

3. Getting a deep insight into how this position relates to the new start's position.

## What are we proposing

The idea is that if the new start has a good understanding of the challenges of the " Zoo" around him/her, the new start will be better able to perform in their own position.

For example, my student son and his girlfriend both work in a busy restaurant. I was chatting to them about this book and they reflected that it is important for the new waiter to quickly learn a bit about what is happening in the kitchen. The restaurant they work for deliberately places a new start in the kitchen for a short period of time. This exposure significantly improves the quality of service and performance of the waiter and the restaurant. Some reasons why this helps a lot:

- The waiter will be better able to estimate the time it will take to produce a meal, and will know, if an order is placed late in the evening, what the impact will be on the restaurant's back staff.

- The waiter will understand why the soup could be cold and can fix the issue before it is delivered to the table.

- The waiter knows which meals to push when. Some meals place a lot of pressure on the kitchen and when the restaurant is busy and the waiter is asked to recommend something, they would not push these meals, but rather promote the pizzas which are quicker to produce.

- If the kitchen is really busy the waiter can advise the patron, if they order paella, that: "We would love you to experience our paella, it is exceptional, but because it is made fresh, it will take 30 minutes to prepare." This will significantly improve the experience for everyone.

- In the kitchen the waiter can quickly serve up the bread or side salad themselves to speed up the process.

No position in an organisation operates in isolation, so if we are able to give the new start exposure to the role and positions around them, we will significantly assist in developing the ability of the new start to respond to challenges, be proactive, help other team members and improve processes and systems.

## Who should we include in the Zoo?

Well, this varies, depending on the position and the level of the new start position. There are a number of considerations that will drive this:

- The different sections in a department.

- The direct customers of the position.

- The direct suppliers of the position.

- The department or suppliers who are key role players in measuring the performance of the position.

To illustrate the vast range of permutations, we have looked at five different new start positions, but every position and company is different.

*Production Operator in the assembly aspect of an auto factory:*

1. The maintenance team which supports the area in which the new start works.

2. The Operations directly upstream and downstream from the position the new employee is recruited for.

3. The logistics supply function that supports the new start's area of assembly.

4. The role of the quality controller at the end of their specific process.

5. The team leader's role.

*A Debtor Controller position in a consumer goods company:*

1. The accounts department.

2. The creditors department.

3. The sales department.

4. Even time in the trade understanding who the debtors are and the challenges trade reps experience with them.

*The Human Resources business partner, responsible to provide HR services to the commercial division of a large company:*

1. The HR division including:
   a. The training division.
   b. The industrial relations/legal support.
   c. The payroll and administration department.
   d. The medical department.
   e. The security function.
2. The management team of the commercial division, the division head and direct reports.
3. The functions of each of the roles in the commercial division.
4. The union representatives in the division.

*The manager of a branch of a retail company:*

1. The logistics department of the company.
2. The major suppliers.
3. The credit control department.
4. The marketing department.
5. Sales planning department.

*The head of a multinational branch in South Africa:*

1. The different divisions represented in South Africa.
2. The international offices supporting the local branch.
3. The head office leadership team.
4. The key local suppliers and customers.
5. The local business community/chamber.
6. Union leadership.

## So how do we do this?

My suggestions are threefold:

1.  By being very deliberate and planning this part of the Onboarding.
2.  By making the process the responsibility of the new start.
3.  By using frequent one-on-one coaching sessions with the new start to ensure implementation.

*Deliberate planning:*

We propose a simple process. However, it is possible to make this more complex and begin to describe specific competencies. While competencies are useful, they also can be extremely time-consuming and rigid. This process is simple, clean, easy to develop and easy to follow up on.

To develop this plan we propose:

Step 1: List the positions in the same department that the new start will need to know.

Step 2: List the positions/departments in front and behind the position.

Step 3: Identify the other positions which are likely to have an impact on the new start's position.

Step 4: Build a spread sheet. See the example for the HR business partner below:

*Table 3: Extract of the "Getting to know the team spreadsheet" for a new member of the HR department*

| | Position title | Core concepts learned | Sign off Achieved/ not achieved |
|---|---|---|---|
| 1 | IR officer | The union structure<br>Major agreements<br>Typical disciplinary issues<br>Code of conduct<br>Strike code, picketing rules and risk plan<br>Disciplinary procedure<br>Grievance procedure<br>**Many others** | |
| 2 | Pay office | Who are the department members?<br>How is the payroll loaded, by whom, time lines?<br>How many payrolls?<br>How are benefits managed/by whom?<br>What are the options?<br>How is leave managed?<br>Where are employee records kept, by whom?<br>**Many others** | |
| 3 | The production department the HR BP is responsible for | The managers in production – who and what<br>The broad production processes<br>Shift patterns<br>Key equipment<br>The Quality Management systems<br>The safety rules<br>**Many others** | |

Other "Zoo members" could include:

■ The Security Department

■ The company's preferred recruitment agents

■ The company's labour legal advisor

■ The artisan training centre

Step 5:   As the new start acquires the listed knowledge, they get it signed off, either by themselves or by the person who provided the information.

Step 6:   Once every month/two weeks the new start meets their line manager and reviews the records and discusses areas of challenge.

**?** Key "why" questions which will confirm the effectiveness of the "Who is who in the Zoo."

1. **Speed and cost:** How long has it taken to complete the full "getting to know them" plan?

2. **Employee value proposition**: Did this process inspire the new start and build an insight into the company?

3. **Team relations**: Does the new start know who's who in the Zoo?

4. **Psychological contract**: Does the new team member feel part of the team?

5. **Leadership imperative:** By leading the new start through the getting to know the Zoo process, did the leader strengthen the connection with the new start?

# Chapter 8

## Becoming Company Competent

> Assisting the new employee to acquire the competencies to function fully in their new company.

## Introduction

If you think of Onboarding as more than an induction process but rather a complete process, then the process of ensuring that the new start acquires the entire ambit of the position they have been placed in is crucial and perhaps the most important long-term requirement.

This is the process of guiding the new start to the point of becoming fully competent. This may sound, in many cases, as if it is a superfluous act as the person we recruit is supposed to have the skills already. There are very few careers which are "Plug and Play". Almost all positions contain a level of technical generic skill as well as a significant amount of environmentally specific skill.

This was well described by a colleague who told me that because she had a large swimming pool at home and had looked after it for years she was confident that she knew what she was doing with a pool. Then she babysat her brother's pool at the coast which had been neglected for a year. She reflected, "While I was a competent pool person, I needed to be exposed to a new skillset at the coast."

Consider the case of Terry.

Terry was appointed as the national sales manager of a significant passenger car company in South Africa. She had been with the company for a number of years and had proven very competent in effectively leading one of the specialised sales departments. She had been appointed into this new position because she was the best person they could appoint, having also been significantly constrained by transformational challenges.

I was privileged to be asked to coach this exceptional person as she transitioned into her new role. When I met her manager he briefed me that while she has a very strong commercial qualification and that, although the basic financial side of the position was new, it would not take too long to grasp, the real challenge she faced was to step up to the strategic aspects of the position. When I spoke to her about the challenges she faced she was personally extremely optimistic about the prospects, and confident that she would just work hard and master whatever other skills she needed to acquire.

While I have no doubt that this would ultimately have proven to be possible, the reality was that she was being watched by all levels in the organisation and being able to step up was critical for her to develop credibility.

We started deliberately preparing her for the position at a strategic level. We started by unpacking the entire sales landscape and identifying the areas of critical success from a knowledge perspective.

It was clear that she needed to build connections across the entire dealer network and make a list of all the key role players, but for her to be to strategic, there was a lot more she needed to know. Things such as:

- The national sales demographic. The sales spread – who bought what where.
- What the different market segments were.
- What competitors were doing.
- Detailed analysis of the national sales trends across all vehicles for the past five years.
- The company's products – physically experiencing them.
- The competitors' products – experiencing them first hand.
- The current organisational strategy in similar markets globally.

Once we had developed a working list, we began to identify which actions were necessary in order to gain the necessary insight. In our subsequent coaching sessions she would report back on progress and key insights. Fortunately Terry is a very fast learner and was willing to put in the hard yards. Very soon she was finding that she was able to contribute to discussions at a surprisingly strategic level.

With her rapidly increasing knowledge came a range of additional benefits including confidence and respect from peers – some of whom had been working at this level for a long time.

The functional learning each position will require will differ dramatically in terms of hard and soft skills. The important issue is to be able to identify them clearly.

Consider Fasie

Fasie was appointed into a material purchasing position in a very professional, but medium sized, parts manufacturer. He was appointed straight out of the graduate programme of a "blue chip" company. Fasie had achieved a degree in logistics at a leading university and, at the time of appointment, it was felt that we had found a "super star" for future management in a department where we had a lack of graduate skill sets.

His appointment had not thrilled the department as it was felt that, for these positions, there was a need for someone with many years of hard purchasing experience, but we and HR had been able to persuade the line manager that the bigger need was for future talent.

Six months in and there was trouble on the horizon. Fasie's manager was ready to throw in the towel. He had expected Fasie to be able to operate in the position almost immediately. He was, after all, a graduate and he should know how to do the basics.

While Fasie was sharp and learned quickly, his knowledge was limited to a broad strategic insight, rather than hard practical skill. Members of the purchasing department take pride in having several important skill sets. Firstly, they are Excel gurus and can create spreadsheets which are so complex that, if the employee is absent for a few days, everyone in the department becomes nervous as no one is able to work the databases. The other core skill is the ability to manipulate a complex MRP (management reporting programme). The members of the team had all grown up with this system and had been instrumental in its implementation. This system was very customised to the organisation's specific purchasing requirements. The older people in the team liked him: "He is an ok kid", he just is useless.

Fasie did not stand a chance. His great education and strategic insight had certainly not prepared him for the basic elements of the new position. While he had a grasp of Excel, he was by no means a guru. He also had a rudimentary knowledge of MRP Systems; the company's specific systems were not standard. Very quickly the line leader was losing confidence in Fasie.

Clearly, the Onboarding had failed. Fasie was taking too long to acquire the necessary skills and stood little chance of fixing this.

Out of desperation, we sat down and examined what had failed in the Onboarding process and what we needed to do to fix it. These were the results of our reflection.

We had failed Fasie:

> We anticipated ability without checking, in particular, Excel and MRP.
> We had done little to ensure a transfer of skill.
> We had not provided reasonable training.
> We had not checked in with Fasie regularly.
> We had not empowered him to take/demand training.
> We had not placed any accountability on the team to assist him.

Fortunately, the line manager was open to insight on our leadership failures. This is not always the case and this reflection could easily have gone in the wrong direction. Fasie had a probation period and may well not have survived the first six months.

## Becoming company competent

While our past experiences and development will take us to a level of competence, there is a significant step needed by all to really become "company competent". The "Who's who in the Zoo" phase will significantly assist this process, but there is clearly a learning process that will run alongside this and this is what we discuss in this section.

There are a number of principles which underline this process and we, in unpacking them, will expand on the entire process required in this crucial phase.

**The six key principles are:**

1. The line leader is fully responsible for this, the success, of this process.

2. The new start is accountable and the process of taking accountability is part of the Onboarding itself.

3. This is a deliberate process designed to secure an outcome.

4. This process is all about creating a learning environment as opposed to exposure.

5. This process is reinforced ongoingly using feedback and review.

6. This process is built around knowledge transferred from the entire team.

## Principle 1: The line leader is fully responsible for the success of this process.

Yes we are busy, yes the average line leader has their hands full with reporting, meetings and a wide range of management stuff. All of this is true and, without exception, they create a single focus which is not surprising.

During this phase of the Onboarding, however, the leadership role of the line leader is under the spotlight. Or at least it should be, for the following reasons:

- The line leader has appointed a new start, or at least, a part of the appointment was the decision of the leader.

- This new employee is part of the leader's team and the success or failure of the new start is the leader's success or failure.

- The manager's commitment to leading will be a direct reflection of how effective the leader is during the Onboarding process.

- In addition, we must not lose sight of expenses and the investment made in terms of time by the organisation in finding the new start. It is now incumbent on the leader to take control and ensure the return on investment realises into a valuable new contributor.

This, of course, does not mean that the line leader is personally responsible to deliver all the learning transfer. It does, however, mean that the line leader needs to at least:

- Ensure that the new start is fully informed as to what the expectations are.
- Initiate the development of the programme of company competency acquisition.
- Sign off on the entire programme.
- Review progress regularly with the new start.
- Record and take corrective action if the programme is in any way stalling or faltering
- Ultimately approve the conclusion of the programme and exit.

The real world often interferes with these longer-term people initiatives. The leader has a further responsibility to protect this process from being derailed by other organisational priorities. While it may be a great opportunity for the new start to work on a cross-functional assignment, ultimately the new start needs to acquire a set of core organisational competencies as soon as possible and the new start's credibility, as an employee, will be closely linked to this capability.

Other development opportunities are valuable, but as far as reasonably possible these should only be considered once the employee has demonstrated proper company competency. It is the line leader who will ensure that this is fully completed.

## Principle 2: The new start is accountable and the process of taking accountability is part of the Onboarding itself.

The reality is that this is the new start's Onboarding process and the acquisition of competency is the new start's accountability. This does not detract from the leader's role, but there is a difference. In training on this subject it is not uncommon for employees to reflect on how poor the organisation's Onboarding was.

This is a common complaint; however, such criticism may never be used as an explanation for employee competency-acquisition failure. When you sign up for a new position, it goes without saying that there is a learning curve ahead and you, the new start, are responsible to achieve this as soon as possible.

So, how will this work? Well, in an ideal situation, the leader will initiate the process we are going to unpack below. In this case the new start has a responsibility to:

- Apply him/herself to the process.
- Acquire the knowledge and competencies required.
- Be honest about what has not been achieved.
- Give feedback progress, ideally without being followed up on.
- Enthusiastically take accountability.

These expectations should be spelt out to the new start at the start of the process by the leader. They form a formal or informal contract between the employee and the company leader.

Where this ideal situation is not possible, or has not been initiated by the company, the new start remains responsible for the company competency-acquisition process. While this may be a less than ideal situation, the new start will have no option but to acquire the company competencies as quickly as possible and would be well advised to either initiate such a process with their new leader – the logic of which would be very hard to deny – or develop a self-lead process themselves.

Ultimately, the quicker and more efficiently the new start masters the "company competencies", the quicker the start will overcome the "new kid on the block" syndrome and become fully respected as a contributor.

### Principle 3: This is a deliberate process designed to secure an outcome.

Consider the way people develop core skills in sport or the arts. Malcolm Gladwell[10] commented that to become an expert in a field takes 10 000 hours of personal application. While this idea is not grounded in good science, no one would dispute the idea that excellence, in any field, requires practice. This phase of the process includes a number of potential levels of competence acquisition:

1.  Where the new start is a recognised expert in the field he/she is recruited for, they will largely only be required to acquire the skills transfer needed in the new company, *e.g. a skilled electrician will have all the skills required to maintain and install electrical equipment. What the new start will not know is the layout of the electrical infrastructure in a specific facility and the unique and historical installation challenges which are facility-unique.*

2.  Where the new start has shown the potential to perform a function, but is not yet an expert in the field, where there is significant competency acquisition needed to fill this position properly. In such a case there is a much higher need for a detailed and planned competency-acquisition plan, *e.g. where a young high-potential marketing graduate is appointed into a marketing consultant position. While the graduate would have some insight into the position, it should never be underestimated how little real practical knowledge a graduate could have. It is quite probable that the graduate has never worked in a marketing department and would never have been exposed to*

*such basic things as dress code and email response times. While some of these things are common sense, a failure can have real consequences for the new start's credibility.*

3.  Where the new start has been appointed into a position within their field of expertise, one that brings an extended leadership component to it. In "the leadership pipeline" Charan, Drotter and Noel[11] describe the transitions necessary when an employee moves from leader of self to leader of others, or leader of others to leader of leaders. As the new start progresses up this leadership pipeline, they describe an entirely new skill set at each stage. While we will discuss this in more detail in the chapter on leadership Onboarding, research shows that failure in this area has significant consequences for organisational performance and requires special care.

While it is not uncommon for new employees to be expected to work hard to gain exposure to the skills that will make them fully independent contributors to the organisation, this practice has some fundamental flaws which need to be highlighted:

1.  Without a clear plan, "how long" it will take is left in the hands of the new employee. This is flawed thinking on two accounts:

    ■  Firstly, because the new employee is new, "getting an understanding of what I don't know is a challenge". This is particularly real where the new employee is in any way seen as a threat to existing employees, and this fear of a new employee is more commonplace than would be expected.

    ■  Secondly, if the new employee is left with the responsibility of achieving competence, how does the manager place a timeline or measure performance on a self-paced process?

2.  There is a need for existing employees, to some degree, to invest in the Onboarding of new peers. Without a clear plan of how this will happen, the "I'm too busy" factor is a great risk and hard to manage, whereas, if there is a clear plan with time management of peer input, it is easier to manage.

For the new start a structured process can be very motivating. Working towards a competence sign-off is a personal achievement and can be very motivational.

### So how to develop such a deliberate plan?

The size and complexity of putting a new start competency plan together can vary dramatically and will, to a large extent, be influenced by the size, commitment and resources available within the organisation.

Best practice in terms of a competency management system for Onboarding a new employee could include a carefully structured online instrument which is developed for this purpose. Such systems are used by blue-chip global corporates and will have any number of different functionalities. A second option is to link the Onboarding competency management system to an existing company in-house learner management system.

Nowadays it should go without saying that managing a process like this is best run on some type of IT system. The challenge is that in most companies this immediately implies cost and investment. We would like to propose that investing in such a system is a good idea in a very large corporate because it provides integration, historical records and easy access. Where a simpler solution is sought after, irrespective of what system is used, the initial setup of even a manual system will require a few hours of personal effort by the leader.

In this section we look at an easily implemented, simple option, not because it is the only option, but because it is the type of option which should be available to all organisations, or even to all managers, who are committed to Onboarding effectively, but do not have good internal support.

This option considers the following principles:

1. It needs to be low cost.

2. It needs to be easy to put together.

3. It should not take days to assemble.

4. It should be repeatable.

5. It should provide good follow-up systems.

6. It needs a level of transparency.

7. It should be able to accommodate any number of Onboardings.

### What process should the company/line leader use?

*Our suggestion is that the most important aspect of this process is to get started, so start with using whatever you are most comfortable with, especially if you are currently sitting with a new, or recently started employee and are ready to take Onboarding seriously.*
Once you have tested the process and identified what works and what does not, you are ready to begin to add some bells and whistles.

The simplest tool available could be an Excel spreadsheet. However, we would like to propose that, as this is a time-based process which has very specific deliverables and outcomes and needs ongoing progress measurement, a simple project management tool should be considered. Most companies have access to some software, but if this is not available, there are many simple project management apps available.

As we will not be using all the functionality of a full project management system (for instance the budgeting and resource management and critical pathing aspects), we just need a system that can manage a simple Gantt chart and record a long list of competencies allocating timing and collaboration. It ideally includes an email progress and reminder system.

### How to generate the competencies

This is the process of developing a list of everything the new start will need to know in order to perform the specific function. Do not forget that you will have already exposed the new start to the structure of the larger organisation and the functions within their new department. During this phase we are talking about the job itself, paying attention to the company-unique elements which would not have been part of any past education or experience.

One of the best sources of such information would be a past employee. Ideally, we should ask such a past employee to develop such a list for us based on their experience. This professional type of handover process should be a standard expectation of a professional person with a level of conscientiousness and should be a standard part of the exit process. In practice, however, this does not happen nearly as often as it should.

If you are starting from scratch and do not have such a commited previous employee, the process we suggest is to put a small team of employees together that have experience in the position and to lead a brainstorming session.

While the leader can do this by him/herself, a team will provide multiple insights which could result in a more complete process. Further, the psychology of jointly building the competency list contracts each participant into the process.

What we are looking for is a granular process where the depth of variety of job functions is unpacked in some detail. At the end of this section we provide a list of possible topic areas to guide the brainstorming.

We suggest that you consider using a simple a process like this:

1. Introduce the job you are unpacking.

2. It may be useful to discuss the purpose/the why of the job, to stretch ideas.

3. Ask the team to generate all the things that they think such a person would need to know to be effective (use a flip chart).

4. List them without questioning or discussing.

5.  If the ideas dry up, use the topics in the attached section to stimulate further ideas.

6.  Once you have generated as many as possible, ask the group to identify which of the ideas are most crucial to be acquired first – vote and sequence.

7.  Once the sequencing has been done, you would estimate the time it would take to acquire each competency and who would be the most suitable person.

8.  There is some merit in looking at the related performance expectations – i.e. generate an invoice in five minutes.

9.  If you have an Excel spreadsheet or a project plan Gantt chart you are now able to put the plan down and set timings.

Such a process should not take more than two hours to do and the result could make a significant impact on the effectiveness of Onboarding.

## Principle 4: This process is built around knowledge transfer from the entire team

Bringing a new employee into the department has a special dimension. Every department has its own unique culture and workflow. There is often some level of history around the vacancy and the appointment, including some level of professional jealousy.

It is really important that the leader manages this dynamic with a level of care and insight. The entire team must be given a briefing around the Onboarding process, what is intended, and its importance in terms of the five imperatives: speed, EVP, the psychological contract, the team cohesion and the leadership relationship.

Each team member needs to be well acquainted with their role and the expected output. Where a buddy or mentor, as discussed in Section One, has been appointed, it is really important that this person then actively gets involved in the development of this process.

The other key aspect at this point, is to identify and recognise "gurus". Rather than forcing the transfer of knowledge from a reluctant employee, the appointment of "guru" experts shifts the focus and gives formal recognition to a skill level. This can help to neutralise the resistance factors.

By allocating responsibilities and delegating components of the process to different team members, we not only spread the workload and give recognition to different levels of expertise, but we also build a level of accountability for the success of the Onboarding to the entire team.

## Principle 5: This process is all about creating a learning environment as opposed to exposure.

There is a significant difference between giving employees exposure and creating a learning environment. We have all probably had an experience of someone showing you a difficult application on your phone, an exercise, explaining a recipe or receiving directions from a stranger. What appeared to be easy is not at all so when you try to do this yourself. It is almost impossible and you really have no idea where to start. This is the difference between exposure and learning.

It is especially so when exposed to practical things; at best, what you learn is what the output looks like – what the standards are. Consider the following true story.

---

**"The problem with gurus"**
**Yoliswa and the packaging machine**

Yoliswe has just been appointed as a packaging machine operator. The machine costs a million Rand and is a reasonably complex thing to run. Fortunately for Joe, the supervisor, he has a multi-skilled operator called Fazel who has run the packaging machine for years as well as many of the other pieces of equipment in the factory. On her first day on the job, Yoliswe is introduced to Fazel as follows and told that Fazel is the absolute guru when it comes to operating the equipment and she is very lucky that Fazel has agreed to help her.

---

Fazel, like most people who have reached a level of "guru status" in the company, is only too pleased to be given the job. Yoliswe is taken over to the packaging machine and Fazel promptly takes off the cover of the machine – which is normally not permitted, except by the guru. Fazel explains to Yoliswe how the machine works and lists a range of impressive technical names and tolerances. He then puts the cover back on the machine and briefly explains the operating sequence. Job done. Fazel wishes her luck and goes back to his station at the other side of the factory.

The inevitable happens when Yoliswe arrives on day two. It does not take her long to make some fundamental mistake and the packaging machine breaks down. During the ensuing crisis, Joe is hauled over the coals by senior management and when it is discovered that this was Yoliswe's first day on the job, the heat just increases. Fazel is summoned and asked if he has trained Yoliswe as had been requested. "Of course," he says. "I showed her absolutely everything – I don't think she is too bright."

Can what happened to Yoliswe happen to others? Absolutely. It happens all the time and not only on the factory floor but in almost all environments. Sadly, in many cases, the new start becomes the victim of organisational neglect. Often it is just unthinkable that the "guru" could be at fault. However, most of us have experienced something like this to a greater or lesser degree.

Could it have been resolved? Of course it could, and without any difficulty.

There is a significant difference between designing an exposure experience and creating a learning environment.

Achieving learning is far more than just showing me how it's done. The challenge when transferring new competencies to a new start is that most often current employees do not really comprehend the difference and once they have carefully shown the new start how to do something, for many, their obligation has been exercised and their job is done.

We could dedicate an entire book to how to implement workplace learning for "gurus". For now, we would like to make the following observation:

"A workplace guru should only be recognised as a guru if they are as good at helping others to learn new competencies as they are at executing the competency themselves."

Where we have workplace competency, especially if the competency constitutes some degree of competitive IP, then investing in teaching the specialist employee makes sense. The speed at which the new start acquires the skills, understanding and knowledge to become fully competent is as much to do with the organisation's ability to transfer knowledge as it has to do with the attitude and ability of the new start to learn.

For learning to take place there are some fundamental conditions that need to be present and need to be understood by all involved in the Onboarding process. In the table below we will unpack these conditions and also provide a checklist question which could be used for introspection by the line leader or HR expert regarding the effectiveness of the learning process.

*Table 4: Fundamental learning conditions*

| Learning condition | Rating<br>1. Not done<br>2. Just present<br>3. Achieved<br>4. Mastered |
| --- | --- |
| *Learning condition 1. Create a safe space to learn.*<br><br>Because of significant development in "brain science", we are Increasingly gaining an insight into how we learn and the effect of the conditions in which the learning takes place.<br><br>Stress and confidence are now known to be significant contributors to how effective learning will be. In the case of teaching a new employee a new competency which is company-unique, there is a lot of merit in assessing the stress conditions which the new start will experience in order to learn. | |

Traditionally, the sink or swim approach is the approach that would be applied here, but there are a lot of reasons why that is not a good idea. We know that people perform well under a moderate level of stress; for the new start there could easily be a level of stress that is beyond optimism – for example, when the new start is encountering, for the first time, new competencies in the high-risk real environment with real consequences. We suggest that carefully considering the environment in which the learning takes place is a first critical step towards effective learning. The following reasons drive this thinking:

1.  As speed of learning is crucial, we need to make sure that this environment is as conducive and effective as possible.

2.  We need to ensure that the learner views the learning process as a positive experience.

3.  The focus on the importance of the competency acquisition in itself provides focus and inspiration to the rest to the team of the importance of this process.

The real issue here is to create a learning environment, as opposed to an exposure experience.

These safe learning environments can be relatively easy to construct. Here are a number of examples:

1.  Many auto companies, these days, provide an entire offline training environment where the new start is exposed to all the fundamental skills sets required for effective online performance, prior to being allowed onto the line. These environments are often built in the production areas.

2.  In non-production environments such simulations are not as easy to construct. This, however, does not mean that this cannot be done. Take a "company art standard" PowerPoint presentation. This is an increasingly demanding requirement. A new staff member could be given several

stretching presentation examples to complete to standard. Then, when the new start is asked to create a real "company standard" presentation, where the stakes are high, and failure would expose the employee, the new start should be ready.

3. Simulations are an extremely effective way of acquiring very specific core competencies. These are normally used to train complex skills cheaply – skills which would be very expensive to aquire in the real world. For example: long-haul driving simulation, flying simulation, weapon simulation, welding simulation and robotic simulation.

4. Dummy systems are ideally used when training a new start in company-unique IT systems. This would include ERPs (Enterprise Reporting Systems), in-house recording systems, as well as complex Excel models, CRM systems (Customer Relationships Models), any form of PLC or robotic system and any other similar system where an incorrect entry would immediately create a record which could destabilise the real live data.

   While setting up such a dummy environment can be time consuming, "deep ending" a new start on an important live system can create far more significant consequences.

5. Role plays: there are some things which are hard to simulate using real environments, but very necessary. Role plays are very effective tools to practise key skills in a safe place. Common use of role plays is for things such as sales calls and pitches, presentations, company disciplinary processes, performance management interviews and any other similar human interaction.

6. Close supervision: where safe learning environments are not possible and the new start is required to work in the real environment from the start, there is the "guru" who needs to work really closely with the new start.

While the traditional "sink or swim" approach is able, to some level, to achieve learning at a psychological level, there are some real possible consequences which must be considered.

The impact of failure with real business or organisational consequences is significant. The new start can cause real losses, lose personal confidence and can experience a loss of peer support.

### Learning condition 2. Training must be learning focused:

*"In a world where training has become increasingly accepted as a valuable and necessary investment, there is a deep responsibility to ensure that training investment really produces the purposes it was intended for."*

## "All investment in training and development is a waste unless one thing happens, and that one thing is Learning."

It is hardly a given that if we do training, learning will be the automatic consequence. Significant research, as well as all our personal experiences, would testify to this. Most of us know the experience of attending training and discovering that after the intervention, even if was a good experience, we actually recall very little after a while.

There is a real danger that, unless there is careful attention to making the learning effective, our investment, ultimately, only achieves a fraction of the intention and results in considerable waste and frustration.

Consider the following:

- Would you ever be able to learn how to ride a bicycle purely from watching a video and never getting on a bike?

- How long would you remember how to assemble an engine if you only read the manual?

- How many people's names would you remember 10 minutes after the first introduction and how long would it take?

While some of us are good at this stuff, these questions highlight how the match between what we learn and how we learn it, is so important. It is based on how we learn and not on content or delivery recognition.

Fortunately, there is a simple guide which has been exceptionally well researched and stands a significant chance of improving the outcome of aligning the learning content and the method of learning.

At a very fundamental level, all learning could be classified in terms of three categories:

1. Things we need to remember: **Memory**
2. Complex and interlinked things we need to understand: **Understanding**
3. Things we need to do in order to learn them: **Doing**

This system of learning analyses was developed by Sylivia Downs in her book *Learning at Work: Effective strategies for making things happen.*[12]

In summary, the use of this tool is based on the simple analysis of what is to be learnt.

1. If the thing to be learnt is something which would need to be remembered (M), the method of instruction should be designed to achieve this. Methods such as acronyms, associations, memory cards and signs can help. Repetition can work as well, but can be an irritation.

    - Examples of things that require this type of learning in the Onboarding context could include: telephone numbers, a start-up sequence, the 10 points on a checklist, the names of all 12 people reporting to me, the security code to the entrance of the main office.

2.  Then there are those things which are more complex and which require some level of understanding. While, commonly at school, we are taught this stuff by our teacher, research shows that **discovery** is a far more powerful learning activity than teaching when **understanding** is the objective. So, asking the learner to study a process, to document it and then to explain it to you, will be far more effective that just letting a "guru" teach it to someone.

    For example, my son was doing a engineering internship in a big auto plant and on the second day of the internship, he arrived at the workstation and found a PLC on his desk with a note on it saying "FIX ME IAN!!!" He reflected to me that this was an awesome learning experience and he was extremely proud to report that he had nailed it by lunch time. During that process he learnt a ton about diagnostics, the basic functioning of a PLC, the power sources and the electronics.

    Understanding is the crucial step between knowing a subject field theoretically and being able to apply that knowledge in the new workplace.

    Unless we are dealing with a very simple process, most organisational processes and systems require a degree of understanding and may require extensive competency acquisition.

    The challenge, as a leader, is to find learning methods which encourage discovery. Discovery is the key ingredient. This, immediately, implies that the guru can play a huge role, but only provided that the guru understands that the guru's knowledge is of little value at this stage and that the ability to turn the learner into a guru, ultimately, will require that the learner, himself/herself, goes through a process of self-discovery.

3.  Then, of course, there are the skills which require muscle memory and a level of brain and body connection. In this case the learner will need to physically **do** the activity.

    Doing is active, it is involved and it requires practice, for example: Some time ago I learnt how to mould pots in a ceramic studio. After a quick demonstration, I sat down at the wheel and I confidently thought that I could do this as easily as my instructor could. Well, that was an exercise in humility and having sprayed myself, my teacher and the rest of the class with clay, I understood that this was a skill that would take time. My theoretical knowledge of ceramics had no value in this situation. I needed to practise.

The other truth is, in this context, that some of us learn certain skills quicker than others and that sometimes it is less about speed and more about quality.

Our workplace is littered with things which we need to master through practical experience; the use of different IT programmes, machines we need to operate, sell, fly a drone, drive a forklift truck etc. Practical skills are not exclusive to any specific level of work. Activities such as the ability to do presentations, chair meetings, do performance interviews and develop a strategy are all practice-based processes. Many of them require both understanding and doing components.

> *The point is that not one of the MUD components of learning would recommend exposure or teaching as a first choice methodology.*

*Learning condition 3. Creating great learning methodologies:*

Every Onboarding activity creates different opportunities for developing great learning methodologies. This is the integration of understanding the content planned to Onboard the new start with an analysis of the type of learning required – as discussed above.

In other words, once a list of competencies has been developed, which the new start will need to achieve full Onboarding, a MUD analysis should be able to give you a good insight into how to set up this process.

So, working with the available "gurus" you may have in your department and the training for learning principles, should not be too complex to assemble a training plan which is not just an "exposure" thing.

How to do this practically – select a topic, for instance, the new start needs to learn how to initiate an invoice on the company Enterprise Resource Planning system (ERP):

■ Ask the Topic Guru what the new start will need to do on the ERP invoice processing system, which is:

    i.   Remember – for instance, the six steps to processing the invoice.

    ii.  Understand – for instance, how the ERP integrates all business processes across the system and when an invoice is initiated on the ERP, a range of other actions flow from that action – a forecast is generated, a customer check is completed, a VAT provision is initiated.

    iii. Do – the new start will physically complete the invoice initiation on the system correctly.

■ Once this has been identified, ask the guru to explain how he/she will achieve each element of MUD, which is:

    i.   Memory – I will give the new start a printed memory card with the six steps recorded which she could refer to if she forgets.

    ii.  Understanding – I will ask the new start to draw a diagram of how the initiated invoice will link to a range of activities across the system. To prompt this, I will suggest she asks someone in the materials department to tell her how the invoice process impacts on their function.

| | |
|---|---|
| iii.    Doing – I will give the new start five dummy invoices to fill in every day for a week. Once the new start has done 25 perfectly, I will begin feeding her actual invoices to process.<br><br>The objective will be to build something special. A process which will do more than just transfer competencies, but also impact on the employee's relationship with the team, the company and the new start's new leader. | |

## Principle 6: This process is reinforced ongoingly using feedback and review

A real challenge in implementing a process like Onboarding is that, while it is hard to put together and it requires some effort, most people would find the development process somewhat stimulating and, especially the first time, the energy levels to make this happen are likely to be high at the outset. However, as time goes on and priorities shift, this initial energy could well fall away and if we do not recognise and manage this risk, the entire process turns into just another good idea, a "flash in the pan".

In the case of an Onboarding initiative this loss of focus over time is extremely dangerous for the simple reason that:

"If we have communicated our commitment to an Onboarding process

to a new start and then lose interest

– this is a breach of promise."

The consequential risks lie in the impact on the leadership relationship, a lack of employee engagement and some damage to the employee value proposition.

So, what to do? While there are possibly several solutions, which will vary depending on the organisation's culture, the following are suggested as fundamental:

1. Ideally, as we do not want to make this process in any way punitive, it is important to reinforce the process and recognise success. If the organisation has accepted that the line leader is accountable for the Onboarding of their new starts and, ultimately, that this process is a success on all five imperatives, it would seem appropriate that the effectiveness of such a new start Onboarding would form part of the performance review of the line leader. This can be done simply and a wide range of feedback loops are possible, but of most importance is the experience of the new starts themselves.

2. While the line leader is the crucial component to achieve success, so too is the new start themselves. The measure of the new start's commitment to this process is fundamental. We would like to suggest that the new start is given:

■ Clear outcome and review instructions: what and when. In some companies this includes a probation period and review process.

■ The new start is empowered to initiate follow-up activities, so if they do not happen, accountability starts with the incumbent themselves. The idea that employees need to take accountability for their own development is generally a sound principle.

3. The HR department also has responsibilities to oversee the process and, if this is a company-enforced process, to play an audit role to ensure implementation.

Practically we suggest that at least a monthly review process is set up between the line leader and the new start and that this review is done using the plan described above to monitor progress.

Once this review has been completed, the project document is forwarded to HR for review.

We further suggest that a more detailed review is conducted between HR, the line leader and the new start examining progress and effectiveness. This should take place at the end of the "first days" phase and a month prior to the end of any probation period. I think that further bi-monthly sessions would be ideal.

## In Conclusion

In previous sections we have highlighted the importance of introducing the new start as early as possible to the company and the department. All these phases of Onboarding are vital if we are to achieve the objectives: Speed, Psychological Contract, EVP and build the leadership relationship.

If we fail during this phase, however, success in the earlier phases is meaningless. We live in a world where fast-tracking talent and nurturing younger generations, assisting them to become company competent should be a line leader's pride and viewed as a real test of their competence as a leader of others. The next section will further highlight the importance of this mindset.

# Chapter 9

## Onboarding People into Leadership Positions

| Building leadership influence.

## Introduction

For me the most exciting coaching assignments I have been involved in have been coaching leaders at the time of taking up a new assignment. There is a dynamic in this moment which has huge significance and risk. A successful leadership Onboarding can produce spectacular results and a neglectful new leader Onboarding can equally fail dramatically.

Taking up a new leadership position could be an extremely challenging process, or a very rewarding and empowering process. While a few leaders seem to be able to step into a new position seamlessly, most new leaders find the process unsettling. The challenge of acclimatising to a new organisation and function is challenging enough, but in the case of the new leader, how to cope with the Onboarding process can have long-term consequences for the leadership relationship. Consider James's experience.

**A leadership Onboarding lesson**

James had developed a reputation as an extremely competent sales executive, with a long track record of a successful sales function at a range of leading dynamic, medium-sized, local companies. When he was headhunted to head up sales at a very competitive local company, on all accounts he was forecast to be a real asset to his new organisation.

His Onboarding had been surprisingly well planned and he was very well received by everyone, in particular, his new team who were extremely excited about his appointment, having operated for some time with a caretaker director.

As fate would have it, within a week of arriving in the organisation, James found himself pulled into the crucial planning process of a whole new product range which would set the tone of the future of the organisation. As the CEO – a very hands-on, very difficult person – was intimately involved in this project and as the nature of the project fell largely within James's skill set and had little to do with the rest of the sales division's current activities, James took the decision to "run with the project".

He largely allowed the sales division to focus on the current business. He thought that this would be a gesture of leadership and that it would show his new team that he trusted them as well as being prepared to shoulder some of the work himself.

The project turned out to be more complex than anyone had imagined and combined with the CEO's very robust leadership style, James found himself working very late every evening and then having to present to a project stand-up meeting every morning. The net result was that the project only really settled down some three months into his new role.

James then started to get himself involved in his new department and, to his horror, he found that the goodwill he had experienced during his first introduction to the department, had totally disappeared. His team were close to outright hostile and the respect that was first evident had disappeared completely. He quickly found that this resistance and respect deficit was also doing the rounds in the company network.

This was a major setback for James, who took his positive leadership profile very seriously. He could not understand what had gone wrong and what had caused this dramatic shift in support.

With the help of a coach, James spent some time in deep reflection about what had gone wrong. This was not an easy process and his final insights were a shock to him. He had a strong personal image of being a strong natural leader, who built dynamic relations with others quickly and effectively. His leadership ability had a reputation of being way above average, but in a short three months, he had dropped the ball completely. The conclusions he came to were that:

- At the start of his new position, he had been accorded the "normal amount of credibility" most leaders could expect at the start.

- This, however, should not be misinterpreted as "authentic trust" but rather "suspended judgement".

- James further reflected that the decision to leave the team to largely function independently was not viewed as an act of leadership, but rather neglect, and after three months this had begun to fester into a level of hostile resentment.

- What was of even deeper concern was that James's authentic people focus and strong "likable" personality was, after three months' absence, seen by his subordinates as inauthentic and manipulative.

- It was also clear that the rest of the organisation was taking a cue from the sales division and therefore his image, across the organisation, was negatively affected.

James began a very slow process to re-establish his relationship with his subordinates. This was not going to be fixed through a team-building exercise or a dinner together. Trust was the issue and trust is not a simple dynamic which can be resolved through a touchy-feely intervention. Further, if now he suddenly began to take interest in the activities of the team and tried to add value, this could well be interpreted as micromanagement.

In James's case, sadly, the damage was so severe that while he had some success at re-establishing a relationship with the team over time, he found that his overall leadership image, across the organisation, was hard to rescue. Some months later he was headhunted based on his past reputation and he moved on. While leaving was perhaps the best option for both him and the organisation, it did leave some scars not only on James (not least from a waste of time perspective), but on his employer as well.

While the Onboarding of a new leader includes all of the five standard drivers we have examined across the previous chapters, the Onboarding of a new leader brings into focus two additional imperatives which are fundamental to the new leader's speedy and successful integration into the organisation.

The additional two drivers are, firstly, developing leadership influence with the new team and, secondly, developing effective 360 degree influence across the organisation. We will briefly touch on the five basics in the context of new leader Onboarding and then place extra focus on the new additional aspects.

## Speed and cost

While speed and cost are key drivers in all Onboarding contexts, when appointing a new leader, they become even more significant. This may seem counterintuitive as departments are often able to function for longer without a manager than a critical skill. If you are purely appointing a manager, that is, someone who will "plan, organise, delegate and control", then perhaps sometimes, without the manager in full control, space could be provided for employees to feel enriched and they may even take up an improved level of initiative, especially if there is a level of skill and professionalism already evident in the team. However, this is not always the case.

If the intention was to appoint a leader, a person who will create an environment where employees thrive, an environment where employees are inspired and achieve beyond their personal self-belief, a transformational leader, then there should be little argument that, the sooner the leader is fully Onboarded, the better.

Research shows that, for an authentic trust relationship to develop between follower and leader, takes time. A subordinate's level of trust is largely the consequence of a positive experience of their leader over time. A level of trust is at the heart of the type of leadership emerging as the only effective option for companies facing the challenges organisations are experiencing as our wider environment evolves into the 4th Industrial Revolution and we learn to cope with continuous change which is volatile, uncertain, complex and ambiguous (VUCA – the acronym describing nature of change in the current age). This is covered in some detail in the introductory section on the leadership imperative driving the importance of Onboarding in chapter 1: "Why Onboarding?"

## Building a team

John Maxwell coined the phrase "the 360 degree leader", essentially highlighting that an effective leader ideally is:[13]

> "Someone who guides and influences their immediate team members and becomes so respected *and* admired that they have influence with everyone in the organisation."

When Onboarding a new leader there are at least three levels of team development which should be considered:

*Figure 2: Three levels of Team Integration*

Three levels of team integration:

1.  The new team that the leader has been appointed to lead, will be dramatically affected by the experience of change and this shift should not be underestimated. We will discuss this in more detail below.

2.  The new leader becomes a member of a team, all reporting to the new leader's leader – the Management Committee colleagues, the sales management team, reporting to a sales director. This integration will be the focus of this discussion.

3.  The new leader becomes a member of the "leadership "of the organisation and, as such, forms part of the wider team of leaders across an organisation. Some of these leaders may be part of their own functional area, they may form part of the input functions upon which the new leader will depend or they may be part of the output customer chain for which the new leader will provide product support or services. Not unlike the need for the new leader to become quickly integrated into their functional team, it is equally important that they quickly become accepted as a part of the wider team. It is also very possible that a new

leader will quickly become part of a cross-functional team and again, the integration into such a team is important, not only for the leader, but the entire project team.

When you consider the case study of James, his integration into the teams he was required to be a part of, became a key challenge. The consequence of a flawed Onboarding process was that while he was at first well received, ultimately, he never fully became accepted or a part of the organisation and ultimately, in James's case, this became a crisis.

While some people are born with a naturally well-developed level of emotional intelligence, which will certainly assist this process, there is too much at stake to leave the process of Onboarding the new leader as a member of the team, at any level, to relying only on their EQ. A good Onboarding process will include a range of deliberate initiatives which will support this happening.

When coaching a new leader through a transition of this nature, we have found that the most effective, but simplest, tool is to guide the new leader through a deliberate process of regular reflection on their 360 degree integration:

1.  The new leader should construct a list of the teams they need to integrate into.

2.  They should then identify the various individuals in each team who are impactful and set up a deliberate and continuous reflective process assessing how the integration is developing with each team and the possible action that could follow. When working with new leaders, we do this in a structured way, using a documented table as a thinking guide.

3.  We review progress regularly.

There is no reason why such a deliberate process should not become part of the Onboarding process of a new leader, with or without a coach. For instance, the appropriate HR person could be used as a sounding board, or the natural mentor, or "support Buddy".

# Employee value proposition and psychological contract

It is probably assumed that a newly appointed leader would arrive open and willing to quickly build a level of organisational loyalty and commitment. Without question, as with all other employees where the Onboarding process has been well planned and executed, this goodwill should translate into a strong company EVP and psychological contract, but this should not just be assumed.

Talented employees with a level of experience in other companies and other company cultures, can be very quick to assess the strengths and weaknesses of an organisation's culture. The new leader, like every other new start, will be subconsciously assessing the quality of their decision to shift companies and their level of "organisational fit".

While we expect senior people to just "get on with it", to "start up and running", a well-designed Onboarding process for senior people will provide a safe environment for them to integrate and acquire skills.

As was illustrated in James's experience, the period of Onboarding also contains significant risk which contracting to an Onboarding process could alleviate. Yes, the leader will, to some extent, need to carve out their own path, but if there is an established Onboarding process in place much less is left to chance.

2. The new start manager

1. The leader of
the new start

3. The new start's team.

*Figure 3: Onboarding leadership challenges*

## The leadership moment (the role of the new start's leader)

In sections to follow we will look, in some detail at the Onboarding leadership role of the new employee/leader. Throughout this book, however, we have referred to a leadership moment where the manager of the new start establishes his leadership influence during Onboarding. This "moment" is even more critical when Onboarding a new leader as opposed to a skilled employee.

We are in this case referring to what Charan, Drotter and Noel[14] called the "Leader of Leaders" in their book *The Leadership Pipeline*. They describe how a leader progresses up an organisation; they shift from being a leader of others (a leader of people who are not in leadership positions), to a leader of leaders, where the leader becomes responsible for people who are leaders themselves.

At each level up at an organisation, the leader becomes increasingly responsible for the quality of the leadership below them.

For this new start's manager, the leadership accountability, during the Onboarding process, is fundamental. This manager is responsible for the quality of leadership which is occurring below and, given the power of the Onboarding process, this manager has an unique opportunity to dramatically impact, during Onboarding, on his or her management team in terms of leadership.

In this case, we are suggesting that the new leader takes direct accountability for the Onboarding of their new start and ensuring that the new start quickly acquires the competencies required by the position to be filled, as outlined thus far in this book.

However, as the "leader of leaders", the manager has the additional opportunity and, we believe, responsibility to ensure that the new start practises a leadership style which is in line with the organisation's and the leader's leadership culture.

The art is: how to do this effectively? As each leader is different and each will practise, to some degree, a different leadership style, we would prefer to emphasise some areas of focus and encourage the "leader of leaders" to find the best way to put them into practice themselves.

## Focus areas for the "Leader of Leader" to put into practice during Onboarding of a new leader

This table lists some principles to be considered – it is suggested that the manager of the new start considers these principles and considers actions which would bring the principles to life in practice. (The manager referred to in this table is the new start's manager.)

*Table 5: Focus areas for the leader of leader*

|  | Principles | Actions |
|---|---|---|
| 1. | The Manager has a clear understanding of the leadership culture he/she is striving to develop in the department/ organisation. | |
| 2. | The Manager takes direct accountability for the new start's Onboarding. (Specific responsibilities can be delegated.) | |
| 3. | The Manager introduces the leadership culture during each phase of the Onboarding process:<br>■ Land the fish<br>■ First days<br>■ Get to know the giant<br>■ Who is who in the zoo<br>■ Becoming "company competent". | |
| 4. | The Manager sets up specific leadership, as opposed to KPI and Management discussions with the new start. | |
| 5. | The Manager monitors the effectiveness of the new start's leadership and provides feedback. | |
| 6. | The Manager exposes the new start to organisational/external leadership training. | |

Three key principles underpin the development of leaders at any stage during the Onboarding process:

- The Manager as "leader of leaders" needs to take **deliberate steps** to ensure that the new start understands the organisation's leadership culture.

- The Manager's most important tool in achieving a leadership impact on the new start is through taking up an active **"coaching role"**.

- The new start, like all managers, learns more about their personal leadership ability through personal **reflection** than any other input. Thus, during the coaching role, the Manager of the new start, or any other manager for that matter, should create or stimulate as many reflection opportunities for the new start as possible.

A manager who has subordinate leaders reporting to him/her, has a significant opportunity during Onboarding to shift culture. Such a manager should not underestimate how bringing in "new blood" into the leadership space has the potential to have a knock-on effect with the entire leadership group.

Rather than seeing Onboarding as a chore or a hassle, Onboarding provides a real opportunity for the manager to build change and shift thinking.

## The additional drivers when Onboarding a new leader

Certainly, from the above, it is clear that when Onboarding a new leader, the drivers which make the Onboarding process so important for an employee or highly skilled professional, are equally important for Onboarding a new leader. However, when an organisation begins to consider their leadership capacity and capability as a key element of organisational structure and an enabler of competitive advantage, the Onboarding of new leaders gains a shift in importance.

These additional elements are focused on activities the new start's leader should initiate, as opposed to something the organisation, HR department or their new manager would initiate. These elements are, however, not automatically intuitive. As a result, assisting the new start to understand their importance in providing such a framework, is essential.

In this context, however, the leadership role played by the new start's manager as outlined above, is a critical success factor.

## 1. Developing leadership influence with the new team

There is little doubt that a leader's effectiveness within an organisational context lies in the leader's ability to exert influence over their followers.

> "The key to successful leadership today
> is influence, not authority." Ken Blanchard[15]

While a mountain of literature that supports this thinking emerges, a recent discussion on a flight to Johannesburg put it simply.

| Passenger in 3b (senior police general responsible for Port Elizabeth) | Passenger in 3c (leadership consultant) |
|---|---|
| 'So, what do you do?' | 'I am a leadership consultant, you?' |
| 'I am a policeman. So you teach people about leadership.' *(thinks – what kind of a job is that?)* | 'Yes, after 30 years in corporate leadership this seems to be what I am meant to be doing.' |
| 'Ok, so what is leadership?' *(not convinced that I should be encouraging this discussion)* | 'Well, this is probably the most written about question in business, but simply, leadership is about influence.' *(though I was going to catch up on some sleep – anyway this is what I do)* |
| 'What do you mean influence?' *(After my MBA classes, and the real world, he is not going to get away that easy.)* | 'There are many definitions of leadership, but most sound a bit like this: Leadership is the ability to influence a person or a group of people towards a common goal.' *(thank goodness for good old Northouse – now to sleep)*[16] |
| *(Now I've got him)* 'That is all very well, but where does influence come from if it is so key to leadership?' *(this theoretical stuff is of so little use!!)* | *(Oops, this is getting real)* 'That is a really good question. I would say that the single most important contributor to influence is trust.' |
| | 'If I asked you to do something with me and you trusted that I had your best interests at heart and that my judgment was good, how would you respond?' |
| 'I would probably go with you.' *(got you!!)* | *(that was easy)* 'This is the power of influence. The ability to persuade you to do something without using my positional power and commanding you.' |

| | |
|---|---|
| 'Ok.' *(smart ass)* 'So where does trust come from?' *(I don't trust anyone!!)* | 'Ok, so let us first check something. Would you trust someone you had never met or knew nothing about?' *(ok sleep time over – this could be a client – he sounds like more than a policeman)* |
| 'No, I never trust a stranger.' *(What ever!!)* | 'So, you would agree that to trust me, you need to have experienced me?' |
| *(He is not getting away so easily)* 'No, I don't agree. I trusted Mandela but I never met him...' | 'I did not ask if you knew the person, but if you had experienced the person. What kind of person was Mandela?' |
| 'They say he was wise but humble, patient but forceful, forgiving but nobody's puppet.' *(have just read* The Long Walk to Freedom *for the third time)* | 'So, how do you know all of this?' |
| 'From what I have read!! What people said about him!' | 'So, you agree that, in some way, you were exposed to him? And as I said, trust is based on your exposure to someone?' |
| 'Ok, but let us get to the real world. How do I develop trust in Me?? How do I get the power of influence?' | 'Well, what do the people who experience you experience?' *(I wonder who this guy is?)* |
| 'You mean people's trust in me is based on what people experience of me?' *(can it be this easy?)* | 'Absolutely – as you connect with me, you develop an impression about who I am and whether I am trustworthy. It would be my guess that ever since we sat down together, you have been assessing me, just as I you. That is how we find out about each other and develop trust.' *(and now??)* |

| | |
|---|---|
| *(Ok maybe he has a point – can he read my mind?)* 'So, If leadership is about trust and influence and trust is based upon your experience of me, then all I have to do is to ensure that what you experience is positive?' | 'Absolutely'. *(He is really getting it.)* 'So, if you have people reporting to you, what do they experience, how do you behave, do they experience a person like you described Mandela as, or someone who really could not care about them?' |
| *(That is so simple, but deep. I think I'm a good leader, but I wonder what they think ????)* 'I see, thank you. You have given me a lot to think about.' | 'Of course, leadership is not that easy, but without a trust relationship, all you are left with is the power of your position!!' *(Looks like I am going to get that sleep after all.)* |

In summary:

Influence is not a capability in itself which is acquired or earned. It is the product, largely, of the level of trust the follower places in the leader. Consider this:

### *If you trust someone, if you trust that they have your best interests at heart, if you trust that their judgement is sound, then when asked for your support, you are likely to follow them.*

If this is true and logic would seem to dictate so, the question arises as to why you would trust someone. The answer to this, at any level, is that your trust would be based on the experience you have of the other.

So back to Onboarding!!

During the first few months a leader has an unique opportunity to build a lasting level of trust with the people the leader has been appointed to lead. This may happen automatically, based on a warm and dynamic personality, however, building a leadership relationship is far too important to be left to chance. It has been our experience that when a new leader has been coached to take **deliberate** steps to build a relationship with subordinates, they stand are given a much better opportunity to succeed, even with an extroverted persona. This, in no way, means that the leader moves away from their authentic self, but rather that the leader places developing relationships with their team as a priority.

## What do we mean by "taking deliberate action"?

There are some people who we find easy to get along with and with whom we easily build a relationship of trust – people who come from the same background as us or people with whom we share common interests or experiences. However, as leaders, we are not appointed to lead only those whom we naturally like; we are called upon to lead a team of people, irrespective of our personal experiences, the diverse group of people who are appointed based upon their skill set rather than our preferences. In the modern world competitive advantage often comes from the level of diversity in our team.

What does this mean to the new start's leader? It means that building sound leadership relationships with the team we are appointed to lead is important and should be regarded as just as important as becoming competent in the organisational unique competency skills we need to master.

The idea of being deliberate, as opposed to just allowing the leadership relationship to develop and emerge, is grounded in the thinking that leadership is a discipline; a discipline that needs to be placed on the agenda, especially in a world where leaders are tightly managed and the focus is on KPIs and management type deliverables.

Again, as each leader is unique and has their own approach to developing relationships, we are not proposing specific actions but rather suggesting a few focus areas.

## Focus areas for the new leader to put into practice during their Onboarding

This table lists some focus areas to be considered – it is suggested that the new start considers these concepts and considers actions which would bring the principles to life in practice. (The manager referred to in this table is the new start manager)

*Table 6: Focus areas for the new leader*

|   | Focus Areas | Actions |
|---|-------------|---------|
| 1. | Hold one-on-one sessions with everyone from the beginning. Not only those who directly report to you but, over time, with everyone. | |
| 2. | Ask each person who reports to you to take you through their functions and where their areas of focus are. | |
| 3. | The new start leader takes every opportunity to get to know the members of the team:<br>• Land the fish<br>• First days<br>• Get to know the giant<br>• Who is who in the zoo<br>• Becoming "company competent". | |
| 4. | The new start leader creates opportunities to meet the members of the team in informal settings as well as formal ones. | |
| 5. | The new start leader builds credibility by demonstrating their willingness to really listen to their people. | |

| | Focus Areas | Actions |
|---|---|---|
| 6. | The new start leader takes actions to ensure that they do not miss key life events. | |
| 7. | The new start leader constantly and deliberately assesses the level of connection they have with each rapport. | |
| 8. | Leadership moments are events that occur to test a leader's ability and leave a mark on their relationships. During the Onboarding process it is possible that the new leader encounters such. | |

Summary

In conclusion, when a leader Onboards, it is a special moment, an opportunity to do something which will move an organisation forward dramatically. It is also a moment where an organisation can make great use of the moment or lose an opportunity.

Yes, like every other employee, the new start leader needs to be Onboarded – landed, survive their first days, get to know the giant, who is who in the zoo and become organisationally competent.

At the same time, the new start leader also faces the considerable opportunity to build a relationship with the new team they have become responsible for.

Success in this area is a real opportunity to shift the organisation forward. Great leaders are a huge organisational asset and the first days are critical for building a leadership profile. To neglect the Onboarding process of a new start leader is a serious missed opportunity.

The successful Onboarding of a new leader is a significant step towards building a great leadership culture

# Chapter 10

## Conclusion

········································································································

> *Building Leadership influence.*

While we hope that you derived some wisdom from *Onboarding: Strategies for getting employees up to speed faster* this book was never designed to be an academic contribution to the field of HR and the subject of Onboarding. It was rather intended to bring focus to Onboarding as an organisational and leadership imperative. This book is designed to highlight that, while Onboarding is an area where organisations often fail, it is an area where, with some simple planning and effort, it can produce spectacular results.

As there are clearly some good ideas for "the how to" of Onboarding included in each chapter, we are also hoping to achieve the following paradigm shifts:

- When we shift from thinking about the traditional HR-driven induction process as being adequate, to Onboarding as a strategic organisational initiative, there is a whole new range of opportunities available to the new start and the organisation.

- Where we introduce the concept that the line leader derives the most benefit from a successful Onboarding and thus is enabled to shift accountability from the HR department to the wider organisation. This does not suggest that HR does not have a role to play. HR can be the architect, the supporter, the coach and organisational conscience. This is a significant shift for most traditional organisations, however, whether this shift itself is achieved or not, it is important that successful Onboarding is viewed as a competitive advantage issue by the organisation.

- Where Onboarding is seen as a tool to build the leadership relationship and the level of the psychological contract between the new start and the new start's manager and organisation.

- Where Onboarding is seen as defined by speed and efficiency and quickly assists the team to adjust to a new member and to ensure that it returns to optimum effectiveness.

- Where great Onboarding builds the company image, as new starts are the best agents for a new company. Where a great Onboarding is all about building the psychological contract between the new start and the organisation and where Onboarding is seen as an act of leadership, the potential of great Onboarding is possible.

From a practical perspective, dividing Onboarding into each of the five core elements of Onboarding: landing the fish, first days, getting to know the giant, who is who in the zoo and becoming organisational, makes a lot of sense.

While we have suggested various activities and processes for each of the elements, we would recommend that each organisation regards these proposals as guidelines, as opposed to the definitive word on best practice. As organisations examine each element of Onboarding, it should be expected that the unique nature of each organisation – their market, size, structure and culture – would provide unique opportunities which would build on the element and enhance the experience.

We do, however, recommend that when developing an Onboarding strategy, the organisation resists the temptation to develop a single Onboarding process. Each of the five different elements brings different experiences and insights. By using the five-stage process, developing a set of unique interventions with different intended outcomes, is possible.

# Appendix

## 1. Memory exercise

## 2. The new start experience

Use this questionnaire after the new start has been in the position for at least four months.

Ask the new start to use the following scoring:

1. Absolutely disagree
2. Somewhat disagree
3. Undecided
4. Somewhat agree
5. Absolutely agree

| | | |
|---|---|---|
| 1. | **Speed** | |
| | 1. I have quickly learned all I need to know to do my job properly.<br>2. I have the equipment I need to do my job properly.<br>3. I am fully competent and can do the job I was employed to do, as well as the person I replaced – or as expected.<br>4. I have not had to wait for anything. | |
| 2. | **Psychological contract** | |
| | 1. I feel like I am part of the organisation.<br>2. I am very pleased with my decision to join the company.<br>3. I am proud to be an employee of ….<br>4. I am really enjoying my new position. | |
| 3. | **Employee value proposition** | |
| | 1. This member of this company is professional.<br>2. This company really cares about their people.<br>3. This company provides great benefits.<br>4. This company lives its values. | |
| 4. | **Team integration** | |
| | 1. The team has made me feel very welcome.<br>2. The team went out of their way to help me.<br>3. I have a relationship with each member of the team.<br>4. I feel part of the team. | |
| 5. | **Leadership Moment** | |
| | 1. My leader is committed to my Onboarding.<br>2. My leader has made an effort to connect with me and to ensure my success.<br>3. I have learnt that my leader is trustworthy.<br>4. My leader has met with me regularly and formally reviewed my progress. | |

| 6. | **Land the fish** | |
|---|---|---|
| | 1. During the period between signing up and starting, the company made a huge impression on me.<br>2. By the time I started at the company, I knew a lot about the company.<br>3. Before I started in the company, I already felt part of the company.<br>4. The company used the time between signing up and starting to sort out a lot of administration. | |
| 7. | **First days** | |
| | 1. Before I arrived at work on the first day, I was well informed about what to expect.<br>2. Day one was extremely well organised.<br>3. At the end of day one, I felt that the day was really meaningful.<br>4. At the end of day one, I felt very well received. | |
| 8. | **Getting to know the Giant** | |
| | 1. I have a clear idea about the size and scope of my new company.<br>2. I know and understand the company values and vision.<br>3. I know the company products in adequate detail.<br>4. I can name the company's key structures. | |
| 9. | **Who is who in the Zoo** | |
| | 1. I can name all departments, across the company, I need to know.<br>2. I know the people working in them, whom I need to know.<br>3. I know all the main functions in our department. | |

| 10. | **Becoming company competent** | |
|---|---|---|
| | 1. I have developed a list of all the functions I need to become competent.<br>2. My manager regularly reviews my progress.<br>3. I am fully competent in the company's IT systems.<br>4. I am happy that I am able to fully perform the competencies required of this position. | |
| | **Total score** | |
| | **Overall rating (devide by 40 to get average rating)** | |

## 3. Checklist

| | **Actions** | **Required yes/no** |
|---|---|---|
| 1. | Desk | |
| 2. | Office | |
| 3. | Chair | |
| 4. | Pen, stapler, in/out rack, pencil, drawing pins, paper clips, sharpener | |
| 5. | Phone | |
| 6. | Cell phone | |
| 7. | Credit card | |
| 8. | Petrol card | |
| 9. | Name on the telephone list | |
| 10. | Name at security | |
| 11 | Name tag | |
| 12. | Parking allocation | |
| 13. | Canteen voucher/registration | |
| 14. | Bookshelf | |
| 15. | Computer desktop | |
| 16. | Computer screen | |

| | Actions | Required yes/no |
|---|---|---|
| 17. | Laptop | |
| 18. | Log on function | |
| 19. | Email address | |
| 20. | Log on to the MRP | |
| 21. | Flash drive | |
| 22. | Allocation of system memory | |
| 23. | Uniform (per number required) | |
| 24. | Safety shoes | |
| 25. | Safety glasses | |
| 26. | Safety hearing protection | |
| 27. | Safety gloves | |
| 28. | Payroll registration | |
| 29. | Medical aid admin | |
| 30. | Group life | |
| 32 | Pension/provident fund | |
| 33. | Tax registration | |

# Endnotes

1   Ulrich, D., & Smallwood, J. 2007. *Leadership Brand, Developing Customer Focused Leaders to drive performance and build lasting value*. Boston, MA: Harvard Business Review Press.

2   Covey, S. 1989. *The 7 Habits of Highly Effective People: Powerful Lessons in Personal Change*. New York: Free press.

3   Russell, M. 2017. *Strategic Leadership: Managing Things and Leading People*. Retrieved from: https://medium.com/swlh/strategic-leadership-managing-things-and-leading-people-2e6b15650870

4   Northouse, P. 2012. *Leadership: Theory and Practice*. California: Sage Publications.

5   Kotter, J. 1992. *Leading Change*. Boston, MA: Harvard Business Review Press.

6   Kotter, J. 1992. *Leading Change*. Boston, MA: Harvard Business Review Press.

7   Sinek, S. (n.d.). *How great leaders inspire action*. TED Talk. Retrieved from: https://www.ted.com/talks/simon_sinek_how_great_leaders_inspire_action/transcript?language=en

8   Lencioni, P. 2002. *The Five Dysfunctions of a Team: A Leadership Fable*. San Francisco: Jossey-Bass.

9   Smith, J. 2015. *21 things you should do on your first day at work*. World Economic Forum. Retrieved from: https://www.weforum.org/agenda/2015/06/21-things-you-should-do-on-your-first-day-of-work/

10  Gladwell, M. 2008. *Outliers, the story of success*. New York: Little, Brown and Company.

11  Charan, R., Drotter, S. & Noel, J. 2010. *The Leadership Pipeline: How to Build the Leadership Powered Company*. San Francisco: Jossey-Bass.

12  Downs, S. 1995. *Learning at Work: Effective strategies for making things happen*. London: Kogan Page.

13  Maxwell, J. 1989. *The 21 irrefutable laws of leadership. Follow them and people will follow you*. Nashville: Thomas Nelson Publishers.

14  Charan, R., Drotter, S. & Noel, J. 2010. *The Leadership Pipeline: How to Build the Leadership Powered Company*. San Francisco: Jossey-Bass.

15  BrainyQuote. (n.d.). Ken Blanchard Quotes. Retrieved from: https://www.brainyquote.com/quotes/ken_blanchard_307860

16  Northouse, P. 2012. *Leadership: Theory and Practice*. California: Sage Publications.

# Index

www.ingramcontent.com/pod-product-compliance
Lightning Source LLC
Chambersburg PA
CBHW062019200326
41519CB00017B/4852